Beadwrangler's

Hands On Crochet

with Beads and Fiber

by

Lydia F Borin

Jo,
Crochet is
the bead +
fiber connection
Let's Hooked!
Enjoy
Lydia
The Beadwrangler
2001

Bead
Expo
Miami
2001

Copyright© 1997 Lyden Enterprises
All rights reserved. No part of this book may be transmitted in any form or by any means, electronic or mechanical, including but not restricted to, photocopying, recording or by any information storage and/or retrieval system without prior permission in writing from the author.

Designs shown in this book are intended for personal use only. Mass marketing of the designs as finished work or as kits is prohibited without permission in writing from the author.

Instructions and designs in this book have been tested and are presented in good faith, but no warranty is given, nor results guaranteed.

First Edition: Published by Hooty Owl Media, December, 1997

Photography by Terry Drymon
Illustrations and design by Dennis Borin

Borin, Lydia F, 1946-
    Beadwrangler's Hands On Crochet with Beads and Fiber by Lydia F Borin
    ISBN 1-891302-01-9
    Library of Congress Catalog Card Number: 97-77051

                      Lyden Enterprises
                      228 N Sun Court
                      Tampa, FL 33613
                      lyden@ij.net

Dedication

To Sally Lewis who taught me how to crochet and set my course in this grand adventure; to St. Petersburg Museum of History, St. Petersburg, Florida, for inspiration through cataloging their beaded purses; and always, to Dennis Borin, my partner in creating all the Beadwrangler books.

My thanks and great appreciation to Editor, Ileana Somerson, Chief Technical Advisor Virginia Tutterow and technical advice from Sally Lewis and Teresa Barrett. Many thanks to testers Barbara Grainger in Oregon City, Oregon and Virginia Tutterow, Joy Magnon, Marcia Mycko, Cheryl McIntosh and Nancy Silva of the Tampa Bay Bead Society.

Contributing Artists

Glassmakers
  Randal Smith, Crystal Fantasies, Largo, FL: Two vases attached to ***The Dreammaker*** and cabochon for ***Mr. Tentacles***, the squid
  Marilyn Gaizband, Annandale, VA : Jigsaw pieces in necklace, ***Puzzle Pieces and Rings***
  Sage, Mountain View, Arkansas: Eye bead on ***The Dreammaker***
  Cheryl McIntosh, Bubbles Beads, Clearwater, FL: Cabochons on crocheted/loom woven purse, ***Merry Mermaid***

Quilters
  Teresa Barrett and Ruthie Miller, Tampa, FL: Quilted pieces for quilted/crocheted purse, ***Coral Sea Star***

Ceramic Designer
  Nancy Matthews, Bradenton, FL: Ceramic goddess on crocheted/loom woven purse, ***Hidden Secrets***

All titled pieces mentioned above appear in the centerfold of the book, pages 32-33.

Table of Contents

Dedication 3
Contributing Artists 3
Table of Contents 4

Introduction 6
History of Crochet 6

General Instructions 8
Crochet Terms 9

Basic Crochet Instructions 10

Bead Crochet Tips
    Bic Trick 17
    Safety Pin Tracker 17
    Thread for Bead Crochet 17
    Do You Crochet Tight or Loose? 17
    Make Spiral Rounds Meet 18
    Add Shaped Beads to Crochet 18
    Avoid Using Glue with Fibers 18

The Basic Instruction Project
    The Beadacious Bag 19

Bags and Purses
    The Scrumptious Ruffle 21
    The Regal Legacy 23
    The Peach Passion 24
    The Sweet Dream 25
    The Delicious Duo 27

Beads
    The Fiber Bead 29
    The Beaded Bead 30
    The Droparound Bead 31

The Inspirational Centerfold 32

More Beads
    The Pattern Bead 34
    The Shaped Bead 35
    The Tube Bead 36

Table of Contents, con't.

Embellishment Goodies
    The Scrunchies 37
    The Scroodles 38
    The Clusters 39

Designer Projects
    The Borini Bag 40
    The Precious Pearl 42
    The Sculpted Vessel 44
    The Ruby Empress 45
    The Beaded Fairy 48

Bead Crochet Techniques
    Working from a Storage Card 52
    Working from a Spool 52
    Adding and Joining Thread 53
    Pre-stringing Beads 53
    Adding Beads to Crochet 54
    Fastening/Tying Off Thread 55
    Using Auxiliary Thread 55
    Adding Beads between Beads 55
    Preparing Crochet for Attachments 56
    Decreasing Stitch with Beads 56
    Making a Crochet Strap 57
    Making a Braid 57
    Making Bead Loops 57
    Embellishing with Beads 58
    Adding Rings 58
    Covering Rings 59
    Adding Fiberfill 59
    Adding Lining to Bags 60
    Using Buckram and Ultrasuede 60
    Making a Crochet Bezel for a Cabochon 61
    Crocheting Consecutive Flat Bead Rows 61
    Making Crochet Pins and Pendants 62
    Making Crochet Earrings 62
    Making Twisties 62

Bibliography 63
Bead and Fiber Organizations 64
Beadwrangler's Hands On Series 64
Beadwrangler's Bead and Fiber Junction 64

Introduction

About eight years ago, magazine articles and books began to surface with bead knitted purses and how-to instructions which began a revival of beaded bags. I could not work with the tiny needles as they hurt my wrists, so I began looking for alternatives. Then one day my beading pal, Sally Lewis, stopped by my house for a visit. I asked if crocheting with small hooks might be less painful and Sally agreed it might be the answer. She asked if I had any crochet hooks and I found one of my Mom's. Sally sat down in our kitchen and in minutes she crocheted a little fiber bag. She handed me the bag and asked if I wanted to learn to crochet. Do beads have holes? Can fiber be spun? Of course I wanted to learn and went to Sally's home for a lesson. I learned the chain stitch and single crochet stitch. Sally was very patient to teach a lefty since she is a righty. That was the beginning of my crochet experience and I knew I was "hooked." I bought a book with basic crochet stitches and worked my way through them all. I made several purses of yarn and thread and became comfortable with the "hook." When I started to add beads, the world changed for me. I knew this was a new direction in my art; creating little bead crochet purses and objects. I have not experienced any wrist pain from crocheting with beads and using smaller hooks.

Bead crochet is no more difficult than learning other bead and fiber techniques. Try it and you will be hooked. You will only need basic crochet techniques to make all the projects in this book. I continue to learn more about crochet everyday and it just excites me more to think of all the items I will create with each technique I master. I have written this book as an easy guide for bead and fiber enthusiasts to learn and make unique bead crochet designs. I have acquired many reference books for cataloging and studying the history of antique purses. These books have inspired me to design hundreds of mini purses that depict purse fashion of the past and capture the romance we miss in our busy modern life today. Instructions are included for basic crochet, right-handed and left-handed, for beginners and as a reference. If you have never crocheted before, I would advise you ask a friend who crochets to help you get started or go to a stitchery center, yarn or bead store that offers lessons. Learn to crochet from the National Crochet Guild, weaver guilds and related organizations. Get hooked!

History of Crochet

Crochet comes from the French word "croche" or "croc" which means to hook. Crochet is defined as making needlework by looping thread with a hooked needle. The history of crochet is surrounded in mystery and controversy. There are no crochet pieces available prior to the 1800s for dating, but it is believed that crochet in one form or another could have been in existence as early as the 1500s. Crochet is believed to be part of nun's work or nun's lace which included needlepoint lace and bobbin lace for Catholic churches. It is also theorized that some of the lace from tombs in

Egypt were crocheted by twisting pieces of cotton between the fingers and making the loops by hand. Another theory is that crochet evolved from tambour techniques which also uses a hook. The earliest examples of crochet come from Europe. Crochet hooks were made in many shapes, sizes and material. Some hooks had a different size hook on each end. There were also crochet sets that had a handle that all the various size hooks fit in and were placed in a box with an inset space for each hook and the handle.

Crochet became very popular by the mid 1800s. Many patterns were published and special fibers manufactured for crochet use. Crochet sales helped save the Irish from starvation in the 1840s. During the mid 1800s, many of the upper and middle class believed crochet should be enjoyed by the elite and the lower class and servants should stick with knitting for necessities of life and not dally making fancy items that was not their place to wear or display. Articles were written to this effect in magazines and there was an angry backlash written by the lower class. Feuds were fast and furious. It makes one wonder if that is the reason that crochet examples can not be found in earlier work; if they were not necessities and considered lavish, then they were idle work. Even schools that taught several methods of needlework were often forced to leave off crochet because of the danger of experimentation and foolery. Many books for crochet and knitting were produced from the mid 1800s through the 1920s. Filet crochet became very popular from the 1850s on and patterns were created for various decorations in the home. From 1937 through the 1940s there were crochet contests for workmanship design and speed. The 1960s ushered in crochet as an accepted art form and more experimentation in textile art occurred. There were international wall hanging shows, fiber shows and exhibits sponsored by large companies, many offering prizes. Crochet continued in popularity through the mid 1970s and then began to diminish.

Today crochet is zooming to the forefront of fiber art with new materials and designs. A variety of crochet books and magazines can now be found at book stores. Many career women are making soft and romantic crocheted clothing and accessories for wear outside the office. The tiny knitted purses with beads have brought an explosion of interest in knitting and revived the world of crochet and beads. Several books of the 1800-1900s have been edited and are now available with bead crochet and knitting projects. People who never thought of crocheting or knitting before are attending classes or learning through books. In the past, crocheters were known as innovators of new techniques and ideas, so it amazes me that many recent crochet publications state you must follow specific rules when crocheting; no exceptions. I am one of the renegade crocheters and this book offers new ideas and techniques that sometimes break the rules. Your crocheted creations today are the heirlooms of tomorrow. Join me as we make history.

General Instructions

You need to know how to chain stitch, single crochet, double crochet, half double crochet, slip stitch and decrease and increase stitches to make the projects in this book. Required terms and abbreviations are included. The first projects are the easiest to make and the more complex are near the end. Each project includes specific supplies, crochet instructions and a list of techniques. You will also need general supplies:

General Supply List
- spools of Anchor#8 or DMC#8 Pearl Cotton thread or equiv.
- crochet hook size 9 or 10, optional size 11 or 12 hook
- 1 medium twisted wire needle
- 1 sewing and 1 tapestry needle with large eyes for crochet thread
- Silamide or Nymo size A beading thread or equivalent
- 1 sharps needle size 11 or 12
- scissors, small pliers to crunch "bad" beads, a dish for loose beads and adequate lights

For Beginners: Chain stitches are made of loops. Loops are also the stitches attached to chain stitches to make single crochet, double crochet and half double crochet. You will be inserting new stitches into the previous stitches of the last row or round. You can put your hook through the back loop, front loop or under both loops. Use the back loops for the crochet projects unless directions state otherwise. If your stitches are too loose, go under both loops. You may need to go under both loops of double crochet. You should try and keep each line of crochet consistent. Crochet instructions include working in **rounds** and **rows**. Each line of beads crocheted in a circle is a round. Each line of beads crocheted flat is a row.

The first project, **The Beadacious Bead**, includes a guide for beginners and most of the terms are spelled out for clarification to those new to crochet. Be sure to review the tips and all techniques listed with each project before you begin. **The Sweet Dream** and **The Clusters** are projects using rows, all others are worked in rounds. Each project will indicate whether you are making rows or rounds. **The Sweet Dream** requires exactly 17 stitches across in each row of beads and each row of threads for it to work. The **bead** projects must also have the exact number of beads for each round.

All other projects list the approximate number of beads required. I designed these projects so that if you miss a stitch, lose count, add an extra bead or place the safety pin, **Safety Pin Tracker**, pg. 17, incorrectly in any of the projects, it will not matter. Your crocheted items will still look BEADACIOUS and you will have fun making them. You may end out with 5 or more beads than the listed amount. All projects with rounds are set up using chain(s) at the beginning and joining the end with a slip stitch in one of the beginning chains to even the rounds. See **Make Spiral Rounds Meet** (pg.18) for instructions and alternative stitches. **The Fiber Bead** is the only project that spirals and no ch1 is required.

> For each project refer to the instructions on pages 10-16 for the beginning stitch of each round or row unless project instructions state otherwise.

You will see **ADD BEADS** listed in crochet instructions to remind you to add beads. A letter "b" is also included with each stitch to indicate a bead in that stitch; example, 1bsc means one bead in a single crochet stitch. In <u>every</u> project using beads with single crochet stitches, you will pull up your bead before the first yarnover. Projects requiring bead placement in other stitches will indicate where to add beads. See **Adding Beads to Crochet** (pg 54) for more information.

Use any color and type beads you wish for each project; however, changing bead size from the one identified in a project will change the appearance of the item. If you are going to combine the bead crochet into items that need laundering, use beads with permanent finishes such as transparent, opaque, iris and matte. Most lined beads will fade with time and lose color with continuous washing. Use a size 9 or 10 hook to begin. Then try a size 11 or 12 hook. Anchor/DMC also make #80 thread which can be used with smaller beads. Crochet thread #20 can be substituted for Anchor/DMC#8, however, it is a little thicker. Experiment with different kinds of thread and a variety of hook sizes. Either start with the how-to-crochet instructions or move on to the projects. Let's get started!

Crochet Terms

You need to learn the crochet terms listed here. The only <u>abbreviations</u> you will need to learn for the projects in this book are in **bold type**. All other terms will be spelled out to help those new to crochet. I have not seen the term *both loops* identified with an abbreviation in any crochet book so I invented one. All terms are those used in the United States.

Note: You will see the letter "b" included with crochet stitches; "b" indicates beads used in that stitch such as 1bsc = 1 bead single crochet, 1bhdc = 1 bead half double crochet and 1bdc = 1 bead double crochet. Specific techniques and projects provide guidance on bead placement in a stitch. Finally, I use "alternate" instead of "repeat".

Crochet Terms	abv
chain stitch(s)	ch(s)
slip stitch(s)	sl st(s)
single crochet(s)	sc
double crochet(s)	dc
half double crochet	hdc
decrease(-ing)	dec
increasing(-ing)	inc
back loop(s)	bl(s)
front loop(s)	fl(s)
both loops	blps
beginning	**beg**
repeat(ing)	rep
round(s)	rnd(s)
skip	sk
stitch(s)	**st(s)**
turning chain	Tch
yarnover	**yo**

Basic Crochet Instructions

I have included these basic crochet instructions for those new to crochet or need a refresher. I have attempted to stay away from the many crochet terms that are found in other books. I expect many people that work with beads will be trying crochet for the first time and may not be familiar with the terms and abbreviatons. I hope you find these instructions helpful and easy to follow. I guarantee that once you learn these basic techniques, you will have lots of fun crocheting with beads!

Preferred Hand Right-handed or Left-handed
Other Hand The one that does everythng else.
Finger Positions Thumb #1 and pinky #5; #2, #3 and #4 are the fingers between.

Left-handed   **Right-handed**

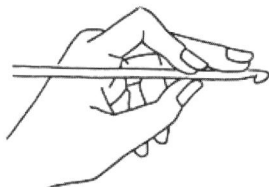   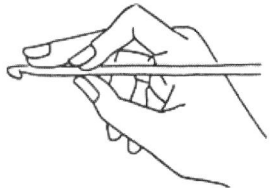

Figure 1

Hold the hook in your preferred hand like a pen as if you were writing a letter. (Figure 1). Turn the hook towards you so that you are facing the fat part where the size and company name are usually listed. Place the hook between thumb #1 and forefinger #2 with #3 finger behind the hook and pressed next to it. Practice each step of crochet with your hands beginning in this position. Hold the hook firmly but not tight. You will use #2 finger off and on as you place the hook into the piece you are working. If this position is difficult, try holding the hook like a knife and put the back portion of the hook to the inside of your hand.

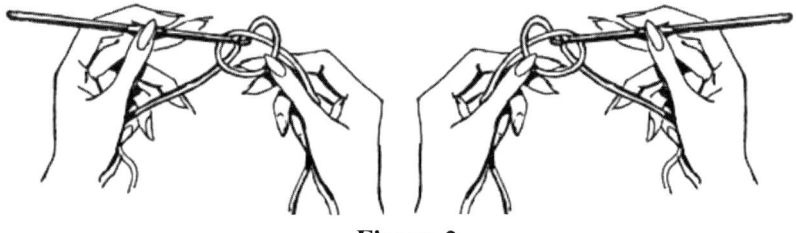

Figure 2

Slip Knot Take theloose end of the yarn and form a loop. Do not tie the loop together or make a knot. Use the hook to pull a portion of the yarn through the loop so you have a circle around the hook and a knot below it. Keep this loop loose until you make the first chain stitch.

Left-handed   Right-handed

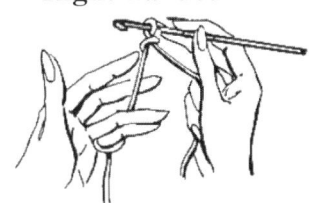

Figure 3

Hand Positon Position your hands so the hook is in your preferred hand. From the hook, transfer the yarn to your other hand, wrap the longer end of the yarn around pinky #5, back up over #4, under #3 finger and over #2 finger. An alternative is to run the thread from around #5, over #4, #3 and #2 for faster thread flow. From the hook, 2" to 3" of yarn should extend to your other hand as the working area. You will also need to hold the short end of the yarn with your other hand. Use thumb #1 and #3 finger of your other hand to grasp the short end of the yarn right under the slip knot next to the hook. (Figure 4)

Figure 4

Chain Stitch (ch) From the side facing you, take the hook under and over the yarn, grabbing the yarn with the hook. Pull the yarn through the loop on the hook. This makes one chain stitch (ch). Now tug on the short end of the yarn so the slip knot becomes taut. The movement of the yarn being placed over the hook is a yarnover (yo). Do not count the loop on the hook as a chain.

 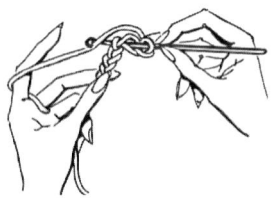

Figure 5

Single Crochet (sc) Make 10 chain stitches and turn the piece to the reverse side. Put the hook through the middle of the 2nd chain from the hook. Then use the hook to yarnover and pull a loop through the 2nd chain.

Figure 6

You should now have two loops on the hook. Now yarnover the hook again.

Left-handed 　　　　**Right-handed**

Figure 7

Pull the yarn through both loops. This is a complete single crochet stitch.

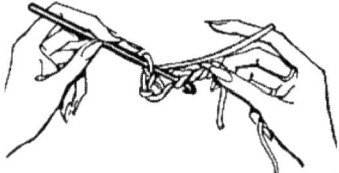   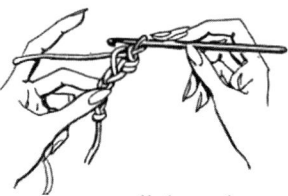

Figure 8

There will still be one loop on the hook after the yarnover pull through.

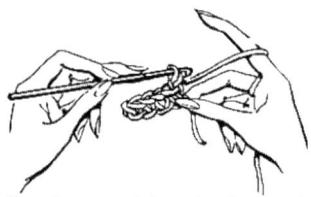   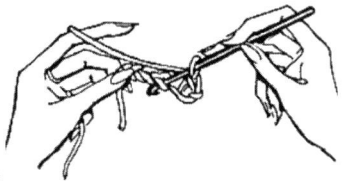

Figure 9

To make another single crochet, put the hook in the next chain stitch and yarnover. Then repeat steps in Figures 6 and 7.

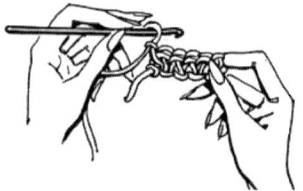   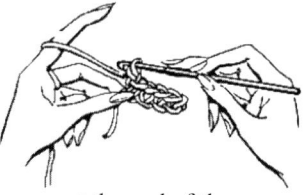

Figure 10

Continue making single crochet stitches until you are at the end of the row.

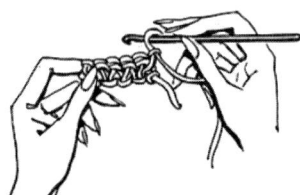

Figure 11

Make 1 chain stitch. This is the turning chain. Now turn the piece to the reverse side. Do not remove the hook when turning the piece. Start the next sc in the first sc of the previous row. ch1 is not counted as a stitch. You yo 2 times to make the single crochet stitch.

Left-handed   **Right-handed**

You can take the hook through the back or front stitch (loop) or under both stitches (loops) to crochet. Stitch placement depends on the crochet item or project. Going under both stitches makes a tighter piece. Going through the back or front stitch makes a looser, stretchy piece and leaves a unique ridge. Most book and magazine projects will state stitch placement. The current trend is to take the hook under both loops. Going through the back loops to make my designs results in wonderful soft textured goodies that everyone loves and begs to touch and feel. Try to keep each line of stitches uniform in stitch placement. Make your sc stitches in previous rows by taking the hook through the back stitch (loop) for the projects in this book unless otherwise instructed in a specific project. Go under both stitches (loops) if your previous row is too loose. Go under both stitches of double crochet and half double crochet when your stitches are too loose. You will need to fasten off when you finish crocheting. See Fastening/Tying Off Thread, pg. 55. Stitch placement in rounds are the same as rows for sc, dc and hdc.

Figure 12

Double Crochet (dc) Make a group of chain stitches first, about 20. Then yo and put the hook through the 4th loop from the hook.

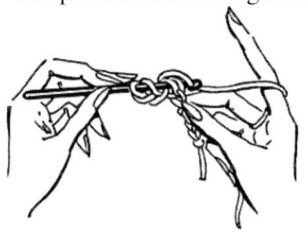 

Figure 13

Then yo again and pull a loop through. There should now be 3 loops on the hook.

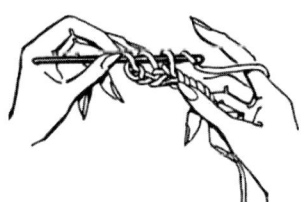 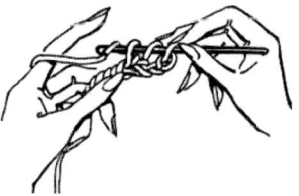

Figure 14

Yo again and take your hook through 2 loops. You now have 2 loops on the hook.

Left-handed   **Right-handed**

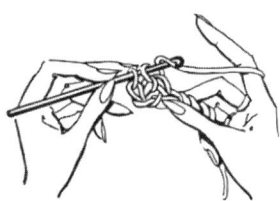 

Figure 15

Now yo again and pull the yarn through the last 2 loops that are still on the hook.

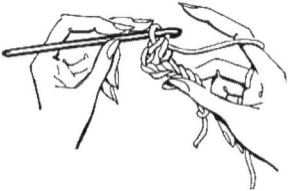 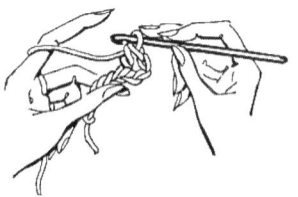

Figure 16

One loop remains on the hook after the last yo. To make the next double crochet, yo, put your hook through the next chain stitch and repeat the steps in Figures 13, 14 and 15 for making the dc stitch. You yo 4 times to make the double crochet stitch.

Figure 17

Continue making dc stitches until you are at the end of the row, then make 3 chains (ch3). Turn the piece to the reverse side. Do not remove the hook while turning the piece. The ch3 counts as the first stitch in a row.

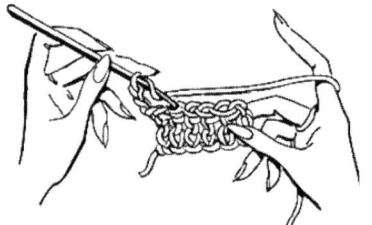

Figure 18

To start the next row, yo, begin in the 2nd dc of the previous row. You may need to go under both loops of dc because the stitches are longer and looser. Continue making dc stitches.

Left-handed **Right-handed**

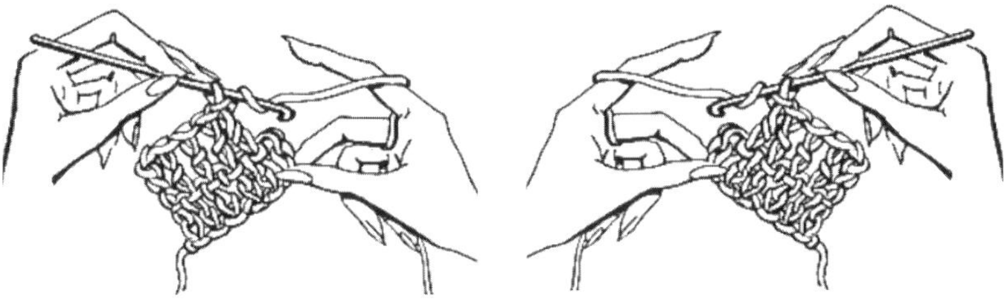

Figure 19

When you are at the end of the row, make the last dc under the top halves of the 3rd chain in the previous row. Then ch3, turn and continue making dc.

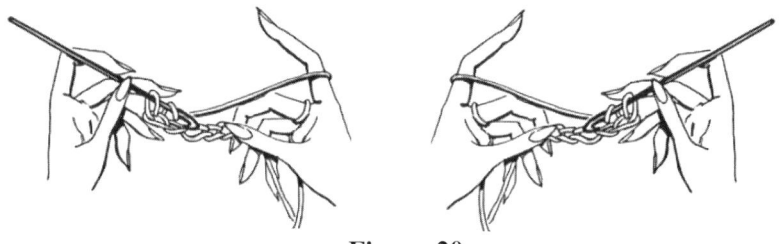

Figure 20

Half Double Crochet (hdc) Make about 20 chain stitches. Yo and put the hook through the 3rd chain from the hook.

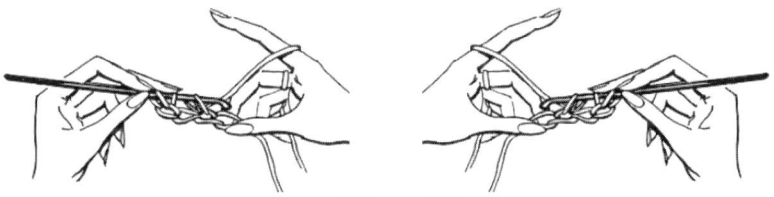

Figure 21

Yo again and pull a loop through. There should be three loops on your hook. Yo again and pull the yarn through all three loops on the hook.

Figure 22

One loop remains on the hook. Continue across the row. Then ch2, turn the piece to the reverse side and start in the 2nd hdc of the previous row. Ch2 counts as the first stitch in a row. You yo 3 times to make a half double crochet stitch.

Left-handed   **Right-handed**

 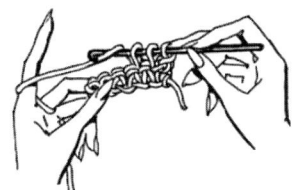

Figure 23

Decreasing (dec) in Single Crochet Put the hook into the next stitch, yo and pull up a loop. You should have 2 loops on the hook. Put the hook into the next stitch, yo and pull up a loop again. You now have 3 loops on the hook. Yo and pull the yarn through all three loops.

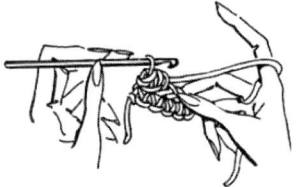 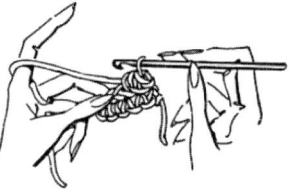

Figure 24

You should have one loop remaining on the hook. For hdc decrease, yo and then continue as in a sc decrease.

Increasing (inc) in Single Crochet Make 2 stitches in the same stitch.

 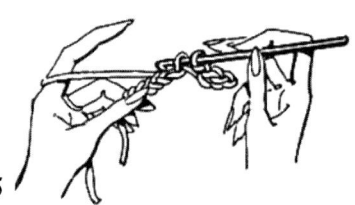

Figure 25

Slip Stitch (sl st) ch10 and put the hook through the 2nd chain from the hook. Yo and immediately pull the yarn through the chain and the loop on the hook. Now make a slip stitch in each chain. Slip stitches can become very dense and tight. ch1 to turn the work. When you begin a 2nd row of slip stitches, put the hook through the back half of each stitch. Slip stitches are used to move the yarn, join pieces, decrease several stitches, as final edgings, decorative stitches and as a closure for some pieces.

Figure 26

Making a Ring Slip Stitches are used to join rings including rounds. ch10 and put the hook through the last ch before the slip knot. Yo and pull the yarn through the ch and the loop on the hook. Continue with choice of stitches.

The Bic Trick

You can use a lighter such as Bic to finish the ends of nylon beading thread. Cut the thread off about ½" from the piece. Hold the lighter near the threads, but let the heat, not the flame, melt the thread. Blow out the flame as soon as the thread has burned and made a bead on the thread ends. Close off the lighter as soon as the thread begins to burn. Parents should be in charge of the Bic Trick.

Safety Pin Tracker

Small safety pins are ideal as round trackers. Make the first round of chains. Join the chains with a slip stitch to make a circle. Then make the ch(s) that precede the next round. Put the safety pin in the top chain. Complete a round of stitches. When you come to the safety pin, remove it and join to the beginning chain. Then repeat the process for the next round. Additionally, attach a paper clip to the written instructions for rounds and rows and keep track by pushing it down the paper as you work.

Thread for Bead Crochet

If you can string your beads on the thread, you can use it to crochet. There are many new threads available for bead crochet. Sewing centers, specialty sewing shops, fabric stores and beads stores carry threads applicable to crochet. Silk, cotton, linen, rayon, fuzzy wool blends and polyester are just a few of the fibers that can be crocheted. Metallic threads can be added in with threads for crochet. When you shop for thread, bring a twisted wire needle and a few beads along. Pull the end of the thread off the spool, thread the twisted wire needle, string a bead and you will know immediately if you can use the thread for your project. Most shop owners will help you with testing.

Do You Crochet Tight or Loose?

If you crochet tight, you may have trouble seeing the stitches when working with smaller hooks and beads. If you crochet loose, you may have trouble with beads slipping through your stitches. I crochet more loose than tight and have learned to tighten more when adding beads. If you will practice with thicker yarn and crow beads first, you will get a feel for how the beads sit and how tight or loose you want to work. Many of my first bead crochet purses had little dents where the beads hid from me. Practice has remedied the problem.

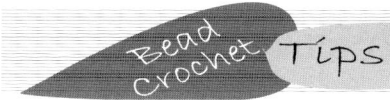

Make Spiral Rounds Meet

Projects with rounds require chain(s) at the beginning of a round and joining the end with a slip stitch in the top beginning chain. This makes each round even. For single crochet, join with a slip stitch in the beginning chain at the end of a round; for half double crochet, slip stitch in the top beginning 2nd chain and for double crochet, slip stitch in the top beginning 3rd chain.

Alternative 1: Spiral the piece. Do not make the beginning chains and work in continuous rounds. Alternating from <u>all</u> bead rounds to <u>all</u> thread rounds and back: Add 2 slip stitches at the end of the last round of all beads or all threads to even the round.

Alternative 2: Combine the last stitch with the top beg ch. For sc, complete 1 yo in the last stitch of the round, then hook into the beg ch, yo again and bring the thread through all the stitches on the hook. For hdc, complete 2 yos in the last stitch, then hook under the top beg ch, yo and pull the thread through all the stitches on the hook. For dc, complete 3 yos in the last stitch, then hook under the top beg ch, yo and pull the thread through all stitches on the hook. This alternative method looks neater but is more difficult to accomplish.

Add Shaped Beads to Crochet

The shape of a bead can alter in appearance when crocheted. You can crochet with any shape bead. However, when you attach it to your crocheted piece, it may look different from your visualization. Several drop beads crocheted together in the round show only the tips of the beads, not the whole shape. Some metal beads are soft like a spring and they may become mashed when crocheted into the piece. Each time you buy new beads with unusual shapes, make a small sample with two or more beads so you will know how they look before you begin a project.

Avoid Using Glue with Fibers

The first place fibers begin to disintegrate is the area where glue was applied. Once the disintegration begins, it spreads throughout the piece. I use a bic lighter or clear nail polish to finish off nylon beading thread. I hold cabochon pieces with my other hand while crocheting or beading a bezel instead of gluing it for ease in adding the bezel.

Bead Crochet Projects

The Beadacious Bag

Introduction

You will make a drawstring bag 1"L x 1" W when closed and 2" wide when open. When the bag is closed, it looks like a fat little bead. The bag is crocheted in a circle that continues in one direction. You will chain(s) at the **beginning of each round**, **not between stitches** unless instructed to do so. Example: ch1. Work 1sc in the first stitch, then 2sc in the next stitch means to make 1 chain at the beginning of the round, not between 1sc and 2sc. Begin each round in the 1st stitch of the current circle, not the chains coming from the hook. Refer back to basic crochet pages 10-16 for beginning placement of stitches. "Work" means to put a stitch where indicated. Read **General Instructions** before you start this project.

Review these Techniques

Working From a Storage Card, pg.52
Working from a Spool, pg.52
Pre-stringing Beads, pg.53
Adding Beads to Crochet, pg.54
Make Spiral Rounds Mcct, pg.18
Fastening/Tying Off Thread, pg.55
Adding and Joining Thread, pg.53
Making a Braid, pg.57
Making Bead Loops, pg.57

Special Instructions

Guide For Beginners If you are new to crochet, I would advise that you purchase a skein of inexpensive yarn and a larger crochet hook such as size G. Purchase yarn that is a light color and easy to see and follow the hook movements. Follow the instructions for making **The Beadacious Bag** and leave off adding beads until you are comfortable making fiber bags and working with the hook. Then string 10mm plastic or glass crow beads on the same yarn and begin crocheting with the beads. You will be able to see what is happening when you crochet and how the beads line up. I made several small bags with thicker yarn first and then added crow beads. Next practice with size 6, 8 or 11 seed beads on thread with a size 9 or 10 hook. If you do not finish with exactly the right number of beads at the end of each round, do not go bead bonkers. Most of us are not engineers or mathematicians; new creations can evolve from mistakes.

Supplies

√ General supply list, pg.8
√ 112 size 6 seed beads

Finishing Touches
Fasten off and sew in loose threads with a sewing needle. You have now crocheted a **Beadacious Bag**. Make a braid and then use a needle to weave it in and out of the double crochet round nearest the bag opening, weaving between two crochet stitches at a time until the braid meets around the bag. Take both braid ends and tie them in a knot. If you had a knot in one end while braiding, take it out before knotting them together. Hold the knot end and pull the braid tight from the end where the bag is hanging, drawing it into a little bag. Pull opposite sides of the bag opening to reopen it. Make decorative knots, embellish with smaller beads or add a crochet bead for the braid end. Make **The Beaded Bead,** pg.30, with 5 rounds of 7 beads, 1 round of 5 beads and 1 round of 3 beads on the end. Chain around the braid below the knot and then crochet the bead over the knot. Use a sewing needle and thread to attach the bead firmly to the braid and tie off.

Variations
Variation #1: Put smaller size beads on the top of the purse opening to see more of the purse fiber. Make sev-

Crochet Rounds for The Beadacious Bag
Pre-string 112 size 6 seed beads using a twisted wire needle.
1 Make 6 chain stitches, then join the ends using a slip stitch to make a circle. (Total-6 chain stitches in a circle)
2 ch1. That means make one chain stitch. Begin with 2sc in the first stitch of the circle and continue 2sc in each stitch to the end. Join with a slip stitch in the beginning chain stitch. (Total-12sc in a circle.)
3 ch1. Work 2sc in each stitch and join with a slip stitch in the beginning chain. (Total-24sc in a circle)
4 ch1. **ADD BEADS**. Work 2bsc in the first stitch and 1bsc in each of the next 2 stitches. Alternate 2bsc in 1 stitch and 1bsc in each of the next 2 stitches until you reach the end and join with a slip stitch in the beginning chain. (Total-32bsc in a circle). Add each bead before 1st yo of the sc.
5 ch1. **ADD BEADS**. Work 2bsc in 1 stitch, 1bsc in each of the next 3 stitches. Alternate and join in the beginning chain. The bead rounds will appear bumpy and stitches will become difficult to see. It will look like more than 2 rounds of beads on the bag. (Total - 40bsc in a circle)
6 ch3. Work 1dc in each stitch and join with a slip stitch in the 3rd chain of the beginning chain. (Total - 40dc in a circle)
7 Repeat Round **6**. (Total - 40dc in a circle)
8 ch1. Work 1sc in each stitch and join with slip stitch in the beginning chain. Go under both loops if you have loose loops from previous dc round. (Total - 40dc in a circle)
9 ch1. **ADD BEADS.** Work 1bsc in each stitch and join with a slip stitch in the beginning chain. (Total - 40bsc in a circle) Go under both loops of the dc.

eral rounds of beads at the top opening using all the same size beads or start size 6's, then make the next round 8's and the last round 11's. You must string all three sizes on one thread and count the number of each size bead, or fasten off after each round and string on the correct size for each round.

Variation #2: Make a bag using size 8 or 11 seed beads with a size 11 or 12 hook. Use 150 size 8 beads or 224 size 11 beads for the same size purse. String the same number of size 8s or 11s as you used of size 6s if you want to use the same crochet instructions and have a smaller purse.

Variation #3: Experiment decreasing and increasing intermittently for a different shape. Make more rounds with beads or more rounds without beads so the purse will look different.

Variation #4: String size 8 or 11 seed beads. Use **The Beadacious Bag** instructions beginning with the first chain stitches. Then make bead loops of 15 beads in each sc stitch of rounds that include beads. This will make a shaggy bag. Make loops of 3 beads around the top of the purse opening.

The Scrumptious Ruffle

Introduction
This is a sweet little drawstring bag with a huge double crochet ruffle around the opening. It looks good enough to eat! You will be making a bag that is 1 ¾"L x 1 ¼"W without the strap and extends to 3 ¼" wide when open.

Review these Techniques
Pre-stringing Beads, pg.53
Adding Beads to Crochet, pg.54
Making a Braid, pg.57
Make Spiral Rounds Meet, pg.18
Fastening/Tying Off Thread, pg.55
Making a Crochet Strap, pg.57
Embellishing with Beads, pg.58
Adding and Joining Thread, pg.53

Supplies
√ General supply list, pg.8
√ 240 size 8 seed beads

Finishing Touches
Fasten off. Cut 3 pieces of crochet thread 12" each to make a small 3 strand braid. String 11 beads on one end, make a bead loop by knotting the thread above it. Use beading or thin sewing thread to sew into the area where the loop is tied and make sure your thread is taut. Then sew around the area above the bead loop and tie

Crochet Rounds for The Scrumptious Ruffle

Pre-string 180 of size 8 seed beads using a twisted wire needle.
1. ch6 and join in a circle with a slip stitch.
2. ch1. Work 2sc each stitch in the circle, join in beg ch.
3. ch1. **ADD BEADS**. 1bsc in each next 3 stitches, 2bsc in next stitch, alternate, join in beg ch.
4-9. Repeat Round **3**.
10. ch3, 1dc in each stitch, join in beg 3rd ch.
11. Repeat Round **10**.
12. ch3. Work 7dc in 2nd stitch and add ch1 after each dc, then work 1sc in 3rd stitch and ch3, alternate, finish with 1sc before beg ch3.

In Round **12** you are making the ruffle edge around the purse opening. You will ch3 as the 1st stitch, then make groups of 7dc in 2nd stitch with a ch1 attached to each dc in that stitch. The 3rd stitch will be 1sc + a ch3 before beginning the next group of 7dc in the 4th stitch.

For a longer purse, make additional dc rounds; for a fatter purse, make additional bsc rounds.

off. Optional: Use clear nail polish for the thread ends. Go to the first set of dc stitches near the purse opening and weave the braid between every 2 dc until you come to the other end, then bring the braid through to the outside. You should have enough braid length to open and close the purse and the loops hang outside. Make a duplicate loop of seed beads on the other end of the braid and tie off. Make a strap for the bag by going to the opposite end from where the braid loops hang. See the illustrations for placement. Bags in the color image have Lark's Head Loops. Make one by doubling the crochet thread on the sewing needle and sew into the side of the purse above the opening, through crochet stitches and make sure your thread is taut. String on 38 seed beads, move the needle across ½" from where the strand end is sewn in. Then sew into the purse until the thread is taut and tie off. Make a Direct Loop for a necklace by sewing the thread farther back from the opening. String 10 seed beads, take the needle into the purse, about ½" forward from where the first end was sewn on, stitch into piece and finish. A Lark's Head Loop is sideways. A Direct Loop is back to front. See illustrations.

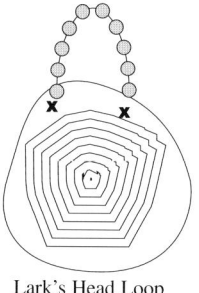

Lark's Head Loop

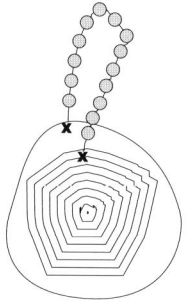

Direct Loop

The Regal Legacy

Introduction
This is a cocoon shaped bag 1 5/8"L x 1 ½"W without the strap. You will be making a bag with cut beads.

Review these Techniques
Pre-stringing Beads, pg.53
Adding Beads to Crochet, pg.54
Make Spiral Rounds Meet, pg.18
Fastening/Tying Off Thread, pg.55
Decreasing Stitch with Beads, pg.56
Adding and Joining Thread, pg.53
Embellishing with Beads, pg.58
Making Bead Loops, pg.57

Supplies
√ General supply list, pg.8
√ 580 size 10 or 11 cut opaque or transparent beads
√ optional,125 size 11 or smaller seed beads for purse rim
√ optional, 1 size 15mm to 20mm ring for Lark's Head purse strap

Finishing Touches
Fasten off. Use crochet thread and sewing needle to make a strap by sewing inside the purse at the top opening until taut. Pull up 70 strung beads on your crochet thread. Sew back into the purse next to the beginning of the strap and tie off.

Now you should have a bead loop which can form a Lark's Head closure for a necklace attachment or use a ring at the end of the loop for attachment. Pre-string 125 or more small beads, attach the hook to the purse rim, work a sc with a 5 bead loop in each stitch. Add all 5 beads before the 1st yo of each sc and join with a slip stitch to the beg ch. Fasten off.

Crochet Rounds for The Regal Legacy

Pre-string 630 size 10 or 11 cut beads.

1	ch6 and join in a circle with a slip stitch.
2	ch1. **ADD BEADS**. 2bsc in each stitch, join in beg ch.
3	ch1. **ADD BEADS**. 1bsc in each next 3 sts, 2bsc in next, alternate, join in beg ch.
4-7	Repeat Round 3
8	ch1. **ADD BEADS**. 1bsc in each stitch, join in beg ch.
9-10	Repeat Round 7
11	ch1. **ADD BEADS**. 1bsc in 1 stitch. Then 1bsc decrease in next 2 sts, 1bsc in each next 3 sts, alternate, join in beg ch.
12	Repeat Round 11
13	ch1. **ADD BEADS**. 1bsc in each stitch, join in beg ch.
14-16	Repeat Round 13
17	ch1. **ADD BEADS**.1bsc in each next 5 sts, 1 bsc decrease in next 2 sts, alternate, join in beg ch.
18	Repeat Round 17
19	ch1. **ADD BEADS**. 1bsc in each stitch, join in beg ch.

The Peach Passion

Introduction

This is a drawstring bag with drop beads on the bottom, rounds of seed beads and the top is crocheted without beads; rings are attached to hang the strap. You will be making a bag 3"L x 2"W without strap.

Review these Techniques

Pre-stringing Beads, pg.53
Adding Beads to Crochet, pg.54
Make Spiral Rounds Meet, pg.18
Fastening/Tying Off Thread, pg.55
Decreasing Stitch with Beads, pg.56
Adding and Joining Thread, pg.53
Adding Rings, pg.58
Making Bead Loops, pg.57
Using Auxiliary Thread, pg.55
Embellishing with Beads, pg.58

Supplies

√ General supply list pg.8
√ optional, add fancy and metallic threads with Anchor/DMC in rounds 12-22
√ 920 size 11 seed beads

Crochet Rounds for The Peach Passion

Pre-string 160 drop beads for first rounds. When finished, remove leftover beads. String 920 seed beads for next rounds. About 200 beads will be leftover after crocheting.

1	ch6 and join with a slip stitch to make a circle.
2	ch1. Work 1 slip stitch in each stitch, join in beg ch.
3	ch1. **ADD BEADS**. 2bsc in each st, join in beg ch. (drop beads)
4-5	Repeat Round **3**.
6	ch1. 1sc in each st, join in beg ch.
7	ch1. **ADD BEADS**. 1bsc in 1 st, 2bsc in next st, alternate, join in beg ch.
8	ch1. 1sc in 1 st, 1sc decrease in next 2 sts, alternate, join in beg ch. Fasten off. String on seed beads.
9	ch1. **ADD BEADS**. Work a 5bsc loop in each st, add beads before 1st yo, join in beg ch.
10-11	Repeat Round **9** and Fasten off after Round **11**. Add thread only and use size 9 or 10 hook if thread is thick.
12	ch1. 1sc in each stitch, join in beg ch.
13	ch3. 1dc in each stitch, join in beg 3rd ch.
14-21	Repeat Round **13**.
22	ch2. 1hdc in each stitch, join in beg 2nd ch.

√ 160 drop beads
√ 6 to 8 size 10mm rings
√ optional; 2 butterflies or other decorative beads

Special Instructions
See **Making Bead Loops**, pg.57, before Round **9**. Put 5 beads together in a loop before the 1st yo of each sc stitch.

Finishing Touches
Fasten off. Sew or crochet rings on the outside of the purse, about ¼" from the purse opening. Space them about ½" apart. Pull up the seed beads left on the crochet thread, about 200, and run them through the rings so you have 4" of bead strap past the purse when drawn. If the beads will not go through the rings, see **The Borini Bag**: Finishing Touches, pg.40. Tie a knot in the end and add decorative knots or add beads over the knot and tie off. Pull the bead strand tight from the purse and you have a drawstring strap. Use beading thread and sharps needle to add decorative beads on the purse above the seed bead loops.

The Sweet Dream

Introduction
This purse is crocheted in one long flat piece instead of a circle. You will be making a purse that folds together and will be 1 ½"L x 1 ½"W on each side. This does not include the purse frame or strap.

Review these Techniques
Pre-stringing Beads, pg.53
Adding Beads to Crochet, pg.54
Fastening/Tying Off Thread, pg.55
Adding and Joining Thread, pg.53
Adding Lining to Bags, pg.60
Covering Rings, pg.59
Crocheting Consecutive Flat Bead Rows, pg.61
Making Twisties, pg.62
Embellishing with Beads, pg.58

Special Instructions
Crochet with size 11 seed beads. After you attach the lining and close the purse, embellish with loops of size 12 or smaller rocaille or cut beads. Each row must have 17 stitches across in bead and thread rows.

Crochet Rows for The Sweet Dream

Pre-string 306 size 11 seed beads. Turn the piece at the end of each row.
1	ch17
2	ch1, turn. 1sc in each stitch across
3	ch1, turn. **ADD BEADS**. 1bsc in each stitch across
4	ch1, turn. 1sc in each stitch across
5-20	Make 8 rows 1bsc in each stitch; alternate with 8 rows 1sc in each stitch. Always ch1 before turning. Remember to **ADD BEADS** in alternate rows.
21-26	ch1, turn. 1sc in each stitch across
27-42	Repeat Rows **5-20** to make the other side of the purse.
43	ch1, turn. 1sc in each stitch across.
44	ch1, turn. **ADD BEADS**. 1bsc in each stitch across.
45	ch1, turn. 1sc in each stitch across. Fasten off.

Supplies
√ General supply list, pg.8
√ 364 size 11 seed beads for purse body, strap and embellishment
√ 370 size 12 to14 cut or rocaille beads for embellishment
√ 1 size 2mm gold bead
√ 2 multiple necklace findings with 5 holes and each measuring 1 ½"
√ optional, 2 plastic rings size 20mm, to cover and use in place of necklace findings
√ optional, fabric scrap: silk or satin material in a light color

Finished Crochet Piece

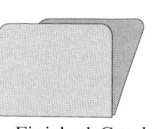

Finished Crochet Piece Folded to Make Purse

Finishing Touches

Now you have one long piece with beads on each end and rows without beads in the middle. See the illustration. For bag lining, see **Adding Lining to Bags,** pg.60. Place the lining over the crocheted side without beads and use a thin needle to tack the edges together, leaving about 1/8" edge around the crocheted piece showing. Fold the purse. See the illustration. Stitch the sides together. Start at the fold area and sew halfway up on each side. Attach each frame by sewing all 5 metal loops to each purse outside edge. At the frame top, put a strand of crochet thread through the metal loop, string 29 beads through both strands. Make a duplicate on the second frame. Tie the strand ends together and make a knot. String the gold bead over the knot. Now use beading thread above the gold bead to embellish with a few rocaille beads and tie off. Use a sharps needle with beading thread doubled and knotted to embellish purse sides. Sew into the purse on one end near the top opening. Make loops of 3 beads along both open sides of the purse and when you are below purse opening on one side begin loops of 5 beads. Continue 5 bead loops around the bottom and up the other side opening and finish with 3 bead loops. Tie off. See **Making Twisties**, pg.62, to add as dangles.

The Delicious Duo

Introduction
You will be making two flat circular pieces and attach them together to make a tiny purse that is 1½"L by 1 ½"W without the strap.

Review these Techniques
Pre-stringing Beads, pg.53
Make Spiral Rounds Meet, pg.18
Adding Beads to Crochet, pg.54
Fastening/Tying Off Thread, pg.55
Making A Braid, pg.57
Adding Lining to Bags, pg.60
Adding and Joining Thread, pg.53

Special Instructions
In Round **7** you will begin with 3ch, adding a bead to 3rd loop of the chain. Then place a bead in each dc after the 3rd yo of the dc. After 3rd yo, pull up a bead and make 4th yo behind the bead.

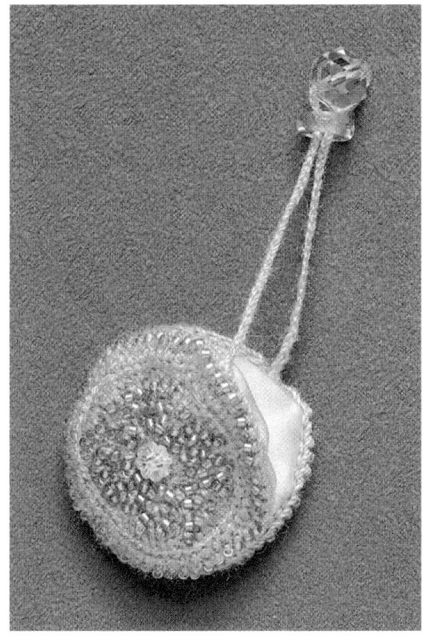

Supplies
√ General supply list, pg.8
√ 336 Delicas or size 11 seed beads
√ 1 size 10mm crystal bead and 1 crystal disk
√ 2 sequins or size 6 seed beads + 2 size 12 or smaller seed beads
√ optional, fabric scrap for lining: silk or satin in a light color

Finishing Touches
For bag lining, see **Adding Lining to Bags,** pg.60. Place a piece of fabric over each of the crocheted circles on the sides without beads and tack them down, leaving a 1/8" edge of each crocheted circle showing. Leave a tiny open space between each circle and the lining at the top, in the middle, to

---

Crochet Rounds for The Delicious Duo

Pre-string 336 size 11 Delica or seed beads. 168 beads make each side.
1. ch6 and join with a slip stitch to make a circle.
2. ch1. 2sc in each st, join in beginning chain.
3. ch1. **ADD BEADS**. 2bsc in each st, join in beg ch.
4. ch1. **ADD BEADS**. 2bsc in 1 stitch, 1bsc in next stitch, alternate, join in beg ch.
5. ch1. **ADD BEADS**. 1bsc in 1 stitch, 2bsc in next, alternate, join in beg ch.
6. ch2. Work 1hdc in each st, join in beg ch.
7. ch3. **ADD BEADS**. Chain 1 bead in the 3rd ch. Then 1bdc in each stitch; add each bead after 3rd yo of each dc, join in 3rd beg ch. Fasten off and then crochet an identical piece.

stitch in the strap before closing the lining. Attach the two crocheted bottoms together with sewing needle and crochet thread. Sew about halfway up each side. Make a 6" braid strap with 3 strands of thread. Sew one end of the braid to the inside of one crocheted piece where the lining is open. String on the disk and then the crystal bead. Put the other end of braid through the disk and sew to the inside of the second crocheted piece and tie off. See the illustration. Tack down the lining that was left open for the braid attachment on each side. Pull the disk up next to the bead to open and pull the disk down to close the purse. Put beading thread on a sharps needle, double the thread and knot the end. Put the thread into the middle of one crocheted circle on the outside and pull thread taut. String 1 sequin and a small seed bead. Take the needle back through the sequin, sew back into the crochet stitches and tie off. The seed bead keeps the sequin attached to the piece. Optional, add bead loops as embellishment along the purse edge.

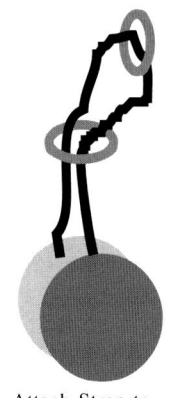

Attach Strap to Inside of Crocheted Pieces

Introduction to Crocheted Beads

All the beads require an exact number of beads for each round. Make sure the beads line up from round to round. Pull up the number of beads required for the current round and keep them separate from the rest of the strung beads. This way you will be sure not to add more or less beads than each round requires. If you begin crocheting a bead and do not have the same amount of beads in each round, then you are not starting out in the right stitch. Each time you begin a new round, make sure you are starting in the same stitch you did in the previous round. If you miss a bead, you can put 2 in one stitch to even it out with the exception of **The Patterned Bead.**

Beads must be pre-strung in an exact order for **The Patterned Bead.** Remember, the first bead strung on the crochet thread is the last bead you crochet. Use a ruler as a guide on the instructions page when stringing the bead pattern.

The Fiber Bead is crocheted in a spiral without a chain at the beginning of each round. You will join each round in the beginning stitch.

The Tube Bead is more difficult to crochet because you have to sc behind beads, a long tube and more beads. See **Making Bead Loops** on page 57.

The Shaped Bead could be made into a necklace. Continue making beads and joining each onto the next. There will be 8 even rounds between each of the fatter bead parts. Finish by joining the ends or add a clasp.

The Fiber Bead

Introduction
The fiber bead is made of variegated rayon yarn thicker than Anchor/DMC thread and embellished with beads. You will be making a round fiber bead with a soft center.

Review these Techniques
Adding Fiberfill, pg.59
Fastening/Tying Off Thread, pg.55
Embellishing with Beads, pg.58

Special Instructions
You will crochet half the bead, stuff it with fiberfill and then crochet the bottom portion of the bead. Spiral the bead round to the next round. Do not chain at the beginning of rounds.

Supplies
√ General supply list, pg.8
√ yarn, 3mm or 1/8" thickness
√ 1 size 00 crochet hook
√ fiberfill
√ optional, 50 size 11 seed beads

Finishing Touches
Fasten off. Embellish the bead by threading a sharps needle, double the thread, knot the end and sew it into the fiber bead until taut. Then string on 3 to 5 beads, lay them flat on the fiber bead and take the needle back into the fiber bead. Come out again, add more beads and continue embellishment. Tie off when finished.

Crochet Rounds for The Fiber Bead

Pre-string. None required. Add beads as embellishment after the bead is crocheted.
1. ch3 and join with slip stitch to make a circle.
2. Work 2sc in each stitch, join in beg stitch.
3. Repeat Row **2**.
4. Work 1sc in each stitch, join in beg stitch. Stuff the bead.
5. Work 1sc in 1 stitch, 1sc decrease in next 2 stitches, alternate, join in beg stitch.
6. Work 1 slip stitch, skip 1 st, alternate, join with slip stitch; Fasten off.

The Beaded Bead

Introduction

The beaded bead is rectangular but can look round depending on the beads used. You will be making a bead that will vary in appearance with each type bead used.

Try various threads, smaller hooks and shaped beads. Use smaller size seed beads. Try beads that are metal, glass, natural and gemstone. Also try disks, rings, gemstone chips, bugles and sequins.

Supplies
√ General supply list, pg.8
√ 60 size 6 or 8 seed beads

Review these Techniques
Pre-stringing Beads, pg.53
Make Spiral Rounds Meet, pg.18
Adding Beads to Crochet, pg.54
Fastening/Tying off Thread, pg.55
Making Bead Loops, pg. 57

More Beads
Bead: Pre-string 80 beads; 8 rounds of 10 beads in each round. **Bead**: Pre-string 60 beads; 10 rounds of 6 beads in each round. **Bead**: Pre-string 15 beads; 5 rounds of 3 beads in each round.

Special Instructions
It is easier to work with a larger number of beads in a round such as 12 and more difficult to work with a smaller number of beads in a round such as 3. It becomes more difficult to see where the hook is and there is less space to work. If you want tight beads without the thread showing, use thinner thread such as topstitching or Conso #69. Go under both loops for a very tight bead.

Crochet Rounds for The Beaded Bead
Pre-string 60 size 6 or 8 seed beads
1 ch12 and join with a slip stitch to make a circle.
2 Work 1 slip stitch into each stitch, join in beg stitch.
3 ch1. **ADD BEADS**. 1bsc into each stitch, join in beg ch.
4-7 Repeat Round **3**.
8 Work 1 slip stitch into each stitch, join in beg stitch. Fasten off.

The Droparound Bead

Introduction
This bead is made of 12 tiny drop beads; each has a hole in the end and hangs like a rain drop. You will crochet one round of drop beads together to form a thin bead to use as a spacer between other beads. Larger textured beads can be made by crocheting several rounds of drop beads together.

Review these Techniques
Pre-stringing Beads, pg.53
Adding Beads to Crochet, pg.54
Make Spiral Rounds Meet18
Fastening/Tying Off Thread, pg.55
Embellishing with Beads, pg.58
Making Crochet Earrings, pg.62
Making Crochet Pins and Pendants, pg.62

Finishing Touches
Make **Droparound** beads for jewelry or add as embellishment. For longer beads pre-string 60 drop beads and crochet 5 rounds of 12 beads in each round.

Supplies
√ General supply list, pg.8
√ 12 drop beads

Crochet Rounds for The Droparound Bead
Pre-string 12 drop beads
1 ch12 and join in a circle with a slip stitch.
2 Work 1 slip stitch in each stitch, join in beg stitch.
3 ch1. **ADD BEADS**. 1bsc in each stitch, join in beg ch.
4 Work 1 slip stitch in each stitch, join in beg ch. Fasten off.

Inspirational Bead Crochet

Items for Future Projects

The Patterned Bead

Introduction
The pattern in this bead spirals. You will be making beads that have a 4 color combination.

Review these Techniques
Pre-stringing Beads, pg.53
Make Spiral Rounds Meet, pg.18
Adding Beads to Crochet, pg.54
Fastening/Tying Off Thread, pg.55

Special Instructions
Pre-string the beads following Pattern I for size 8s and Pattern II for size 11s. There are 9 rounds of 12 beads in each round. Using more beads of one color before changing to the next color decreases the slope of the spiral.

Supplies
√ General supply list, pg.8
√ 4 colors size 8 or 11 seed beads, 27 beads of each color; total = 108 beads

Crochet Rounds for The Patterned Bead

The pattern is shown in the 9 rounds required to make the bead.
Use A, B, C & D to identify 4 different seed bead colors.
Pre-string 108 beads for Pattern I or Pattern II in the order shown working left to right and down the rows.

Pattern I for size 8 seed beads	Pattern II for size 11 seed beads
BBAABBAADDCC	BAAADDDCCCBB
CBBAABBAADDC	BBAAADDDCCCB
CCBBAABBAADD	BBBAAADDDCCC
DCCBBAABBAAD	CBBBAAADDDCC
DDCCBBAABBAA	CCBBBAAADDDC
ADDCCBBAABBA	CCCBBBAAADDD
AADDCCBBAABB	DCCCBBBAAADD
BAADDCCBBAAB	DDCCCBBBAAAD
BBAADDCCBBAA	DDDCCCBBBAAA

1 ch12 and join with a slip stitch to make a circle.
2 Work 1 slip stitch in each stitch, join in beg stitch.
3 ch1. **ADD BEADS.** 1bsc in each stitch, join in beg ch.
4-11 Repeat Round 3.
12 Work 1 slip stitch in each stitch, join in beg stitch. Fasten off.

The Shaped Bead

Introduction
This bead starts with 4 even rounds, increases at the middle and decreases again to 4 even rounds. You will be making beads that look thin on the ends and fat in the middle.

Review these Techniques
Pre-stringing Beads, pg.53
Make Spiral Rounds Meet, pg.18
Adding Beads to Crochet, pg.54
Decreasing Stitch with Beads, pg.56
Fastening/Tying Off Thread, pg.55

Supplies
√ General supply list, pg.8
√ 200 size 11 seed beads

Special Instructions
You can use variegated thread to spiral color mixes; or you can begin with light color beads on one end and work to dark on the other for contrast. You would have to pre-string the beads in a specific order to end with light to dark beads.

Crochet Rounds for The Shaped Bead

Pre-string 200 size 11 seed beads. (#) indicates total stitches in each round

1	ch10 and join with a slip stitch to make a circle. (10)
2	Work 1 slip stitch in each stitch and join in beg stitch. (10)
3	ch1.**ADD BEADS**.1bsc in each stitch, join in beg ch. (10)
4-6	Repeat Round 3. (10 x 3)
7	ch1.**ADD BEADS**. 2bsc in 1 st, 1bsc in next st, alternate, join in beg chain. (15)
8	ch1.**ADD BEADS**.1bsc each next 2 sts, 2bsc in next st, alternate, join in beg ch. (20)
9	ch1.**ADD BEADS**.1bsc in each stitch, join in beg ch. (20)
10-11	Repeat Round 9. (20 x 2)
12	ch1.**ADD BEADS**.1bsc in each next 2 sts, 1bsc decrease in next 2 sts, alternate, join in beg ch. (15)
13	ch1.**ADD BEADS**. 1bsc decrease in 2 sts, 1bsc in next st, alternate, join in beg chain. (10)
14	ch1.**ADD BEADS**.1bsc in each stitch, join in beg ch. (10)
15-17	Repeat Round **14**. (10 x 3)
18	Work1 slip stitch in each st, join beg stitch. Fasten off. (10)

The Tube Bead

Introduction
This bead is made of long tubes and seed beads. You will be making a mini sculptured bead.

Review these Techniques
Pre-stringing Beads, pg.53
Make Spiral Rounds Meet, pg.18
Adding Beads to Crochet, pg.54
Fastening/Tying Off Thread, pg.55
Making Bead Loops, pg.57

Special Instructions
There will be 1 round of 10 seed beads, then 3 rounds of seed beads and tubes combined and then another round of 10 seed beads. Each round with tubes should include 10 tubes. 5 seed beads, 1 tube and 5 seed beads will be looped in each sc stitch. It will become more difficult to see what you are doing as you add rounds because the tubes clump up everywhere. See **Making Bead Loops** on page 57 for instructions to make the loops.

Supplies
√ General supply list, pg.8
√ 30 tubes size 20mm or 25mm
√ 350 size 11 seed beads

Finishing Touches
String your sculpture on a necklace or display it as a sculpture. Make several **Tube Beads** and string on a necklace between other beads. Make **Tube Beads** using smaller tubes such as 5mm tubes and smaller seed beads between the tubes.

Crochet Rounds for The Tube Bead

Pre-string 15 seed beads and 1 tube, then alternate stringing 10 seed beads and 1 tube until all 30 tubes are strung and finish with 15 seed beads.

1. ch10 and join with a slip stitch to make a circle.
2. Work 1 slip stitch in each stitch, join in beg stitch.
3. ch1. **ADD BEADS**. 1bsc in each stitch, join in beg ch.
4. ch1. **ADD BEADS**. Put 5 beads, 1 tube and 5 beads as a loop in each sc stitch before the 1st yo. Continue loops in each bsc stitch, join to beg ch.

5-6. Repeat Round **4**.

7. ch1. **ADD BEADS**. 1bsc in each stitch, join in beg ch.
8. Work 1 slip stitch in each stitch, join in beg ch. Fasten off.

The Scrunchies

Introduction

Scrunchies are made of little bead crochet pieces that spiral in and out; use either side as the front. You will be making little scrunched up pieces for jewelry and embellishment.

Review these Techniques
Pre-stringing Beads, pg.53
Adding Beads to Crochet, pg.54
Make Spiral Rounds Meet, pg.18
Fastening/Tying Off Thread, pg.55
Using Buckram and Ultrasuede, pg.60
Making Crochet Earrings, pg.62
Making Crochet Pins and Pendants, pg.62

Special Instructions
Make smaller **Scrunchies** by using smaller size beads. Make larger **Scrunchies** by continuing to add 2 beads in each stitch in more rounds or by using larger size beads. Use variegated thread for contrast.

Supplies
√ General supply list, pg.8
√ 168 size 6, 8 or 11 seed beads

Crochet Rounds for The Scrunchies
Pre-string 168 seed beads size 6, 8 or 11
1   ch6 and join in a circle with a slip stitch.
2   ch1. Work 2sc in each stitch, join in beg ch.
3   ch1. **ADD BEADS**.2bsc in each stitch, join in beg ch.
4-5 Repeat Round **3** and fasten off.

The Scroodles

Introduction
Scroodles are puffy little bead chains all squeezed together. You will be making **Scroodles** for jewelry, to cover buttons and as embellishment.

Review these Techniques
Pre-stringing Beads, pg.53
Adding Beads to Crochet, pg.54
Make Spiral Rounds Meet, pg.18
Fastening/Tying Off Thread, pg.55
Adding and Joining Thread, pg.53
Using Buckram and Ultrasuede, pg.60
Making Crochet Earrings, pg.62
Making Crochet Pins & Pendants, pg.62

Special Instructions
In Round **3,** make a series of 5bch that become loops. Take each loop down into the next stitch of the main piece, work a slip stitch, then begin the next 5bch until you have a circle of bead chain loops. Do Round **4** the same.

Supplies
√ General supply list, pg.8
√ 165 size 11 seed beads

Crochet Rounds for The Scroodles
Pre-string 165 seed beads size 11
1   ch7 and join with a slip stitch to make a circle.
2   ch1. 2sc in each st, join to beg ch. (Total - 14 sts in a circle)
3   ch1.**ADD BEADS**. 5bch. Work 1 slip stitch in next st on the piece, then 5bch and slip stitch in next st on the piece, continue, join with slip stitch to beg ch. (Total - 13 groups of bead chains in circle)
4   ch1. **ADD BEADS**. 5bch. Take chain into next stitch below first circle of 13 bead groups, begin 2nd group of bch spiraling towards the middle for a total of about 20bch loops and fasten off. Thinner Scroodles: Put 2 sts between each bch loop in the 2nd group = 10 to 14 loops.

The Clusters

Introduction

Clusters look like grapes on vines and can be sewn together as embellishment, made into pins and rope necklaces and even used as separators between beads. **Clusters** are crocheted in flat rows.

Review these Techniques

Pre-stringing Beads, pg.53
Adding Beads to Crochet, pg.54
Adding and Joining Thread, pg.53
Using Buckram or Ultrasuede, pg.60
Making Crochet Earrings, pg.62
Making Crochet Pins and Pendants, pg.62
Crocheting Consecutive Flat Bead Rows, pg.61

Special Instructions

Size 8 seed beads make excellent grape bunches. Grape colors: pink, red, purple, green. Blackberries: red or wine and black. Try various lengths, widths and size beads. The centerfold ring necklace was crocheted using the **Cluster** instructions. Make consecutive flat bead rows and join as an alternative method.

Supplies

√ General supply list, pg.8
√ 60 seed beads size 6, 8 or 11 to make 1 cluster

Crochet Rows for The Clusters

Pre-string 60 seed beads in size 6, 8 or 11

1. ADD BEADS. 10bch.
2. ch1. Turn to reverse side. **ADD BEADS**. 1bsc in each st. Go under both loops.
3. ch1. Do not turn. Take hook across and through 1st st on opposite side. **ADD BEADS**. 1 bsc row in front of crocheted bead row.
4-6. Repeat Row **3**.
7. 1ch. Slip stitch two sides together. Fasten off.

The Borini Bag

Introduction
Borini Bags are romantic and intriguing combining the atmosphere and charm of Mardi Gras in New Orleans, Louisiana, and Venice, Italy, in a tiny dynamic package. The bag shape is reminiscent of larger antique beaded bags and spinning tops made in Venice. Borini is the designated name for the bag in honor of the original Borini family of Venice. You will be making a bag that is approximately 2 ½"L x 2"W without strap.

Special Instructions
See **Making Bead Loops**, pg.57, before working Rounds **12**, **14** and **16**. Add loops of 3 beads before the 3rd yo of each dc. Then finish the dc stitch as usual. In Round **18,** make the ruffle edge around the purse opening with groups of 5dc in 1 stitch and ch1 after each dc, then work 1sc in the next stitch and ch3 before beg the next group of 5dc. In Round **19** turn your crochet piece to make 1bsc in each stitch on the outside ruffle edge.

Review these Techniques
Pre-stringing Beads, pg.53
Adding Beads To Crochet, pg.54
Make Spiral Rounds Meet, pg.18
Fastening/Tying Of Thread, pg.55
Adding Rings, pg.58
Embellishing with Beads, pg.58
Making Bead Loops, pg.57
Decreasing Stitch with Beads, pg.56
Adding and Joining Thread, pg.53

Supplies
√ General s supply list, pg.8
√ 1045 size 11 seed beads
√ 30-35 freshwater pearls or 4mm beads for the middle section
√ 6 size 10mm glass rings
√ 1 decorative disk and 4 mm bead for the bottom of the purse
√ optional, 7 small flowers and 3 tiny metal bugs with holes for attachment

Finishing Touches
Fasten off. String the pearls or 4mm beads, using directions from **Adding and Joining Thread,** pg.53, to attach them around the purse bottom where the first dc round was made. You will

Crochet Rounds for The Borini Bag

Pre-string 890 size 11 seed beads.
1. ch6 and join with a slip stitch to make a circle.
2. ch1. Work 2sc in each stitch, join in beg ch.
3. ch1. **ADD BEADS**. 1bsc in each next 3 sts, 2bsc in next st, alternate, join in beg ch.
4. ch1. **ADD BEADS**. 1bsc in each next 2 sts, 2bsc in next st, alternate, join in beg ch.   *1 bead sc   2 beads sc*
5-8. Repeat Round **4**.
9. ch1. **ADD BEADS**. 1bsc in each next 4 sts, 1bsc decrease in next 2 sts, alternate, join in beg ch.
10. ch3. 1dc in each stitch, join in beg 3rd ch.
11. ch1. 1sc in each stitch, join in beg ch.
12. **ADD BEADS**. ch3 (1 bead in 1st ch, 2 beads in 2nd ch, no bead in 3rd ch). Work 1dc in each stitch with 3 bead loop before 3rd yo of each dc, join in beg 3rd ch.
13. ch2. 1hdc in each next 2 sts, 1hdc decrease in next two sts, alternate, join in beg 2nd ch.
14. Repeat Round **12**.
15. ch2. 1hdc in each next 2 sts, 1hdc decrease in next two sts, alternate, join in beg 2nd ch.
16. Repeat Round **12**.
17. ch2. 1hdc in each stitch, join in beg 2nd ch.
18. ch3. 5dc in 2nd st and ch1 after each dc, 1sc in 3rd st and ch3, alternate, finish with 1sc before the beg ch3.
19. ch1 and turn piece. **ADD BEADS**. 1bsc in each stitch, join in beg ch.

bsc, join and fasten off at the other end. Your purse should puff out now from the bigger beads. Now tie off the crochet thread at the purse bottom. Take doubled beading thread and a sharps needle to stitch through the bottom until taut. String on the disk, 4mm and a seed bead. Take the needle back through the 4mm and disk, not the seed bead, and sew back into the purse. Bring the thread back out near the edge of the disk and string on approximately 25 seed beads. Wrap the strand snug against the disk and sew into the purse next to the disk. If the strand bulks up, take some of the beads off; this strand pushes the disk out a little more for decorative appeal. Tie off. Next go to the **inside** rim of the purse below the ruffle. Attach the hook in the ridge of stitches below the ruffle and follow directions for **Adding Rings**, pg.58. When finished, make a strap through the rings with 128 seed beads on the crochet thread if the rings are large enough

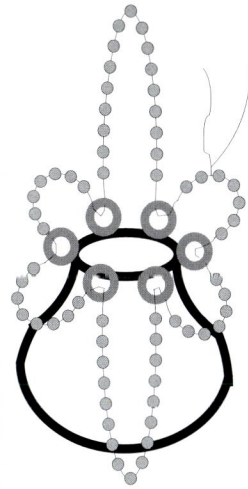

Loops and Rings

for the beads to go through. Tie the ends in a knot. If the ring openings are too small to bring the beads through, string them between each ring; make sure you plan where you want the two longer strands to be as the hanging straps. String 5 beads, go through a ring, string 5 more beads, go through a ring, string on 54 beads, go through a ring, then string 5 beads, go through a ring, string 5 beads, go through a ring, then string 54 beads and remove the needle. Now tie the 2 thread ends with beads together. See the illustration. In either case, use a sewing needle and thread to make decorative stitches over the knot or use a sharps needle and beading thread to add more beads over the knot. Cut both sides of excess thread and tie off. Now go to the middle of the purse above the big beads and embellish with flowers and bugs and tie off. Make a necklace to display your **Borini Bag**.

The Precious Pearl

Introduction
This is a fan shaped purse with optional drawstring. You will make an exotic purse that is approximately 2"L x 3 ¼"W without the strap. Embellish a purchased cord and wear your purse.

Review these Techniques
Pre-stringing Beads, pg.53
Adding Beads to Crochet, pg.54
Make Spiral Rounds Meet, pg.18
Fastening/Tying Off Thread, pg.55
Decreasing Stitch with Beads, pg.56
Adding and Joining Thread, pg.53

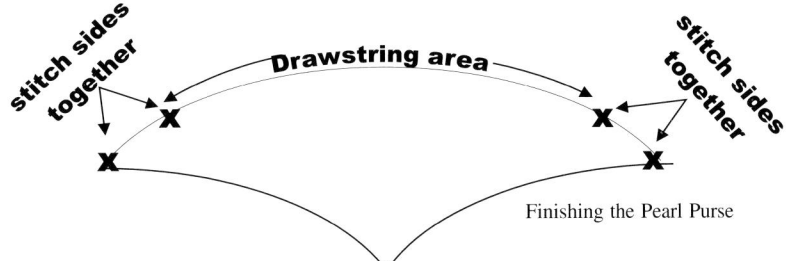

Finishing the Pearl Purse

Embellishing with Beads, pg.58

Special Instructions

In Round **16**, work 3sc in each space between dc stitches. For each sc, go under both stitches of each dc.

Supplies
- √ General supply list, pg.8
- √ 247 freshwater pearls, small gemstone chips or 6mm beads
- √ 1 size 12mm to 14mm silver dangle or decorative bead
- √ 2 size 8mm and 2 size 4mm silver beads
- √ silk thread size E or F, about 12" for drawstring on purse
- √ optional, 40 freshwater pearls for cord embellishment
- √ optional, 15 size 4mm silver beads for cord embellishment
- √ optional, 1 button and about 12" of 2mm cord for cord loop

Finishing Touches

Fasten off. Fold purse in half. Thread a sewing needle with crochet thread and put it through some of the crocheted stitches to anchor it. Bring the needle out to one end that is folded and tack down both sides together, about ¾" in length. See the illustration. Tie off. Go to the other side and

Crochet Rounds for The Precious Pearl

Pre-string 247 freshwater pearls.
1. ch5 and join with a slip stitch to make a circle.
2. ch1. Work 2 sc in each stitch, join in beg ch.
3. ch1. **ADD BEADS**. 1bsc in each stitch, join in beg ch.
4. ch1. **ADD BEADS**. 1bsc and 1sc in each stitch, join in beg ch.
5. Repeat Round **4**.
6. ch2. 1hdc in each stitch, join in beg 2nd ch.
7. ch3. 1dc in each stitch, join in beg 3rd ch.
8. ch1. **ADD BEADS**. 1bsc and 1sc in each stitch, join in beg ch.
9. Repeat Round **8**.
10. ch1. 1sc in each stitch, join in beg ch.
11. Repeat Round 10.
12. ch1. 1sc decrease in 2 sts, 1sc in next st, alternate, join in beg ch.
13. ch1. 1sc in each stitch, join in beg ch.
14. ch1. **ADD BEADS**. 1bsc in 1 st, 1sc in next st, alternate, join in beg ch.
15. ch3. 1dc in 1 st, then skip 1 st, alternate, join in beg 3rd ch.
16. ch1. Work 3sc between each dc st of the previous round, join in beg ch. Go under both loops.
17. ch2. 1hdc in each stitch, join in beg 2nd ch.

do the same. Go to the purse bottom and use thread and needle to sew a big silver dangle bead to the bottom of the purse and tie off. Use crochet thread at the purse top middle area and stitch into the outside edge of one purse side until the thread is taut. Then pull up 30 pearls. Attach the pearls to the other side of the purse on the outside and tie off. Now you have a strap. Take beading thread and a needle and go back through the strap for strength and tie off. Now thread the sewing needle with the silk thread. Take the needle to the dc area right below the purse strap. Weave the needle in and out of the dc stitches, going from the front of the purse to the back and around. Skip the purse sides that you sewed together. When the needle is back to the silk thread in front, string on 1 size 4mm silver bead, 1 size 6mm silver bead and 1 pearl. Then make a knot. Leave about 1 ½" of silk on the end; repeat on the other end of the silk. Twist the silk thread ends open for decoration. This is your drawstring; leave it loose or pull it tight. See **Embellishing with Beads**, pg.58, to embellish a cord with beads and pearls. See the example on the cover.

The Sculpted Vessel

Introduction

This is a mini sculpture. You will be making a little vase that is wide on the bottom, skinny in the middle and increases to a ruffle at the top. It is approximately 1 ½"L x 1 ¾"W.

Review these Techniques

Pre-stringing Beads, pg.53
Adding Beads to Crochet, pg.54
Make Spiral Rounds Meet, pg.18
Fastening/Tying Off Thread, pg.55
Decreasing Stitch with Beads, pg.56
Adding and Joining Thread, pg.53

Special Instructions

Take the hook under both loops where you want the vase stiff and through the back loop where you want the vase floppy. Display the vessel as a sculpture or add a loop and string it onto a necklace.

Supplies

√ General supply list, pg.8
√ 255 size 6 seed beads

Crochet Rounds for The Sculpted Vessel
Pre-string 255 size 6 seed beads.
1   ch6 and join with a slip stitch in a circle
2   ch1. Then 2sc in each stitch and join in beg ch.
3   ch1.**ADD BEADS.** 1bsc and 1sc in each stitch, join in beg ch.
4   ch1.**ADD BEADS.** 1bsc in 1st, 1sc in next st, alternate, join in beg ch.
5   Repeat Round **4**.
6   ch1.**ADD BEADS.** 1bsc in 1 st, 2sc in next st, alternate, join in beg ch.
7-9   Repeat Round **6**.
10   ch1.**ADD BEADS.** 1bsc in 1 st, 1sc decrease in next 2 sts, alternate, join in beg ch.
11-12   Repeat Round **10**.
13   ch1.**ADD BEADS.** 1bsc in 1 st, 2sc decreases in next 4 sts, alternate, join in beg ch.
14   Repeat Round **13**
15   ch1.**ADD BEADS.** 1bsc in 1 st, 1sc in each next 2 sts, alternate, join in beg ch.
16   Repeat Round **15**
17   ch1.**ADD BEADS.** 1bsc in 1 st, 1sc in next st, 2 sc in next st, alternate, join in beg ch.
18-19   Repeat Round **17**
20   ch1. Then 2 sc in each stitch, join in beg ch.
21   ch1. 1sc in each st, join in beg ch. (go under both loops) Fasten off and shape the vase.

The Ruby Empress

Introduction
This little bag has a lid attached that can be pulled up to open and pushed down to close. You will be making a purse that is approximately 2 ¼"L x 1 ½"W without the strap. The lid is ½"L x ½"W.

Special Instructions
See **Making Bead Loops**, pg.57, before working Round **17** of the purse bottom. Add a 3 bead loop before the 3rd yo of each dc and then finish the dc as usual.

Review these Techniques
Pre-stringing Beads, pg.53
Adding Beads to Crochet, pg.54
Make Spiral Rounds Meet, pg.18
Fastening/Tying Off Thread, pg.55
Decreasing Stitch with Beads, pg.56
Adding and Joining Thread, pg.53
Using Buckram and Ultrasuede, pg.60
Making Bead Loops, pg.57
Embellishing with Beads, pg.58

Supplies
√ General supply list, pg.8
√ 700 size 11 seed beads
√ 1 size 20mm glass drop bead and 1 size 4mm matching bead or equivalent
√ optional, 1 disk, flower or decorative bead with hole in the middle
√ optional, 1 size 30mm ring for a rigid purse bottom

Finishing Touches

Make a lining for the lid top by cutting a circle of ultrasuede and buckram that will fit inside. The lining should not cover the hdc outside the lid. Use a sewing needle and thread to sew the buckram and ultrasuede to underside of the lid with the buckram hidden. Attach the hook. Then use crochet thread and make a 6bch on one side, outside the lid edge. Then ch1 and turn, work 1 bead slip stitch in each chain, for a total of 6 beads. Fasten off. Sew the loose end down to the lid so the loop sticks out for the bead strap to go through and tie off. Make a duplicate loop for the opposite side. Use crochet thread to sew into the purse bottom near the opening, through the dc stitches before the 3 bead loop rounds. Stitch into that area so the thread is taut. Pull up 85 beads on the crochet thread. Take the strand of beads through the loop up one side of the lid, over the lid, down through the other loop and back down to the purse bottom. Stitch this end of the strand into the opposite side in the purse edge and tie off. You should be able to move the lid up and down. Double beading thread and use a sharps needle to go through the strap again for strength and then tie off in the bottom piece. At the middle of the lid, string on a 4mm bead on the

Crochet Rounds for The Ruby Empress

Pre-string 580 size 11 seed beads. Begin with the Purse Bottom.

1	ch5 and join with a slip stitch to make a circle.
2	ch1. Work 1 slip stitch in each stitch, join in beg ch.
3	ch1. **ADD BEADS**. 2bsc in each stitch, join in beg ch.
4	ch1. **ADD BEADS**. 1bsc in each stitch, join in beg ch.
5	ch1. **ADD BEADS**. 1bsc in each next 2 sts, 2bsc in next st, alternate, join in beg ch.
6-9	Repeat Round **5**.
10	ch1. **ADD BEADS**. 1bsc in each st, join in beg ch.
11-15	Repeat round **10**.
16	ch2. 1hdc in each st, join in beg 2nd ch..
17	**ADD BEADS**. ch3 (1 bead in 1st ch, 2 beads in 2nd, no bead in 3rd). Then work a 3 bead loop before the 3rd yo of each dc, join in beg 3rd ch. Fasten off.

Now make the Purse Lid with the beads left on your thread.

1	ch5 and join with a slip stitch to make a circle.
2	ch1. Work 2 slip stitches in each stitch, join in beg ch.
3	ch1. **ADD BEADS**. 2bsc in each stitch, join in beg ch.
4	ch1. **ADD BEADS**. 1bsc in each stitch, join in beg ch.
5	ch1. **ADD BEADS**. 1bsc in each next 3 sts, 2bsc in next st, alternate, join in beg ch.
6	ch1. **ADD BEADS**. 1bsc in each next 4 sts, 2bsc in next st, join in beg ch.
7	ch2. 1hdc in each next 2 sts, 2hdc in next st, alternate, join in beg 2nd ch. Fasten off.

lid top, leave a seed bead on the end as the stopper bead and take your thread back through the 4mm and tie off. Do the same with beading thread and sharps needle at bottom of the purse. After the thread is taut, sew to the bottom end and string a decorative bead, 5 seed beads, go through a drop bead, 5 more seed beads, back through the decorative bead, sew into the purse and tie off. Stick a 30mm ring around the purse middle, inside at the very top opening for a rigid edge.

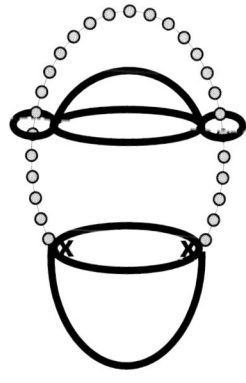

Lid Attachment to Purse

The Bead Fairy

Introduction
Bead Fairies help find beadacious beads. **The Bead Fairy** body, neck and head are all one piece. The arms are crocheted separately and attached. You will embellish her with wings, beads, and other fun stuff. Make Dolls, Angels, Fiber Fairies and Fantasy Figures with just a few changes to the pattern.

Review these Techniques
Pre-stringing Beads, pg.53
Adding Beads to Crochet, pg.54
Make Spiral Rounds Meet, pg.18
Fastening/Tying Off Thread, pg.55
Decreasing Stitch with Beads, pg.56
Adding and Joining Thread, pg.53
Making a Crochet Bezel for a Cabochon, pg.61
Using Auxiliary Thread, pg.55
Embellishing with Beads, pg.58
Making Bead Loops, pg.57

Supplies
√ General supply list, pg.8
√ skin tone thread, size #80 for a petite doll and dress thread
√ 775 size 11 seed beads for dress and embellishment
√ 100 size 8 or 200 size 11 seed beads for hair

√ 60 size 12-14 seed beads for cabochon bezel
√ 6 small drop beads and one large 10mm-20mm dangle bead
√ optional, pair of metal wing/leaf shapes or equivalent with attachment hole

Finishing Touches

Arms: First attach each arm to the upper body, next to the neck, using crochet thread and a sewing needle. Sew the loose thread left hanging on finger of each hand to the stomach area, in the middle. Keep the hands about ½" apart and tie off. **Embellishment:** Use doubled beading thread and sharps needle to attach thread to the inside of one hand, string on 1 seed bead, 3 drop beads, 1 large dangle, 3 drop beads, and about 30 seed beads. Wrap the last portion of strung beads around the 2nd hand and sew under the hand and tie off. **Cabochon Face**. Attach the cabochon with as many crochet stitches as necessary to go around the cabochon with or without beads and fasten off. A button can be substituted as the cabochon. **Hair**: String on beads for hair and attach the hook into the crown area of the head. The number of beads used for the hair depends on how many rounds made and the size of bead used. For size 8s, begin going in a circle with 1bsc in each stitch. For size 11s, alternate 3 to 5 bead loops to build up the hair. Work in any direction to fill in the hair and then fasten off. **Wings:** Take beading thread and sharps needle and attach the wings to the fairy back near each shoulder and tie off. **Decorative Neckline**: String beads on crochet thread for the neckline, attach hook and make loops of 3 or 5 beads in sc around the back, over the shoulders, below the wings, above the chest line and join with a slip stitch. The loops should help keep the wings up. Your **Bead Fairy** is complete. **Angels**: Use white or silver beads and crochet thread. Use crochet or beading techniques and add a strand of gold beads or fiber around her head. **Fiber Fairy**: Crochet the whole doll with fancy fibers and metallic threads. Make a bouquet of tiny needleworked fibers, crocheted, woven, etc., and attach it to her hands. Make wings of fiber over wire and attach them. **Fantasy Figures:** Attach tiny charms or items that depict the character desired and leave off the wings. Experiment and make critter people. **Dolls**: Start at the waist up, crocheting a doll all skin tone, then go from the waist down, increasing at the bottom for a rear end and stitch the end flat instead of round. Fasten off. Then make two legs like you did the arms, beginning with 8-10 chains in a circle, finish, attach and dress her. You can wear a doll by stringing a long loop of beads on crochet thread, take it between the arms and body and around, tie a knot, cover the end with fiber or beads. Attach the loop to a necklace with a Lark's Head closure.

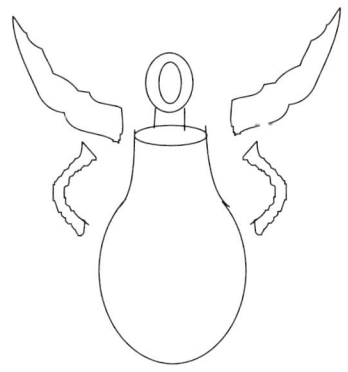

Bead Fairy Attachments

Crochet Rounds for The Bead Fairy

Pre-string 665 size 11 seed beads. Stuff the doll as you crochet.

Making the dress

1. ch5 and join with a slip stitch to make a circle.
2. ch1. **ADD BEADS**. 1bsc in 1 st, 2bsc in next st, alternate, join in beg ch.
3. Repeat Round **2**.
4. ch1. **ADD BEADS**. 1bsc in each next 2 sts, 2bsc in next st, alternate, join in beg ch.
5. ch1. **ADD BEADS**. 1bsc in each next 3 sts, 2bsc in next st, alternate, join in beg ch.
6. ch1. **ADD BEADS**. 1bsc in each next 4 sts, 2bsc in next st, alternate, join in beg ch.
7. ch1. **ADD BEADS**. 1bsc in each next 5 sts, 2bsc in next st, alternate, join in beg ch.
8. ch1. **ADD BEADS**. 1bsc in 1 stitch, 2bsc in next st, alternate, join in beg ch.
9. ch1. **ADD BEADS**. 1bsc in each next 6 sts, 2bsc in next st, alternate, join in beg ch.
10. ch1. **ADD BEADS**. 1bsc in each st, join in beg ch.
11. Repeat Round **10**.
12. ch1. **ADD BEADS**. 1bsc in each next 6 sts, 1bsc decrease in next 2sts, alternate, join in beg ch.
13. ch1. **ADD BEADS**. 1bsc in each next 4 sts, 1bsc decrease in next 2 sts, alternate, join in beg ch.
14. ch1. **ADD BEADS**. 1bsc in each next 5 sts, 1bsc decrease in next 2 sts, alternate, join in beg ch.
15. ch1. **ADD BEADS**. 1bsc in each next 3 sts, 1bsc decrease in next 2 sts, alternate, join in beg ch.
16. ch1. **ADD BEADS**. 1bsc in each next 5 sts, 1bsc decrease in next 2 sts, alternate, join in beg ch.
17. ch1. **ADD BEADS**. 1bsc in each next 6 sts, 1bsc decrease in next 2 sts, alternate, join in beg ch.
18. ch1 **ADD BEADS**. 1bsc in each stitch, alternate, join n beg ch.
19. ch1. **ADD BEADS**. 1bsc in each next 7 sts, 1bsc decrease in next 2 sts, alternate, join in beg ch.
20. ch1. **ADD BEADS**. 1bsc in each next 3 sts, 1bsc decrease in next 2 sts, alternate, join in beg ch.
21. ch1. **ADD BEADS**. 1bsc in each next 5 sts, 1bsc decrease in next 2 sts, alternate, join in beg ch.
22. ch1. **ADD BEADS**. 1bsc in each next 6 sts, 1sc decrease in next 2 sts, alternate, join in beg ch.

23 ch1. **ADD BEADS**. 1bsc in each next 3 sts, 1sc decrease in next 2 sts, alternate, join in beg ch.
24 ch1. **ADD BEADS**. 1bsc in 1 st, 2sc in next st, alternate, join in beg ch.
25 ch1. **ADD BEADS**. 1bsc in each next 2 sts, 1sc in each next 3 sts, alternate, join in beg ch.
26 ch1. 1sc in each stitch, join in beg ch.
27 ch1. 1sc in each next 6 sts, 1sc decrease in next 2 sts, alternate, join in beg ch and fasten off. Attach skin tone thread.

Making the chest and neck
28 ch1. 1sc in each stitch, join in beg ch
29 Repeat Round **28**.
30 ch1. 1sc in each next 4 sts, 1sc decrease in next 2 sts, alternate, join in beg ch.
31 ch1. 1sc in each next 5 sts, 1sc decrease in next 2 sts, alternate, join in beg ch.

Making the head
32 ch1. 1sc in 1 st, 2sc in next st, alternate, join in beginning chain.
33 ch1. 1sc in each next 4 sts, 2sc in next st, alternate, join in beg ch.
34 ch1. 1sc in each stitch, join in beg ch.
35 Repeat Round **34**.
36 ch1. 1sc in each next 4 sts, 1sc decrease in next 2 sts, alternate, join in beg ch.
37 ch1. 1sc in each next 3 sts, 1sc decrease in next 2 sts, alternate, join in beg ch
38 ch1. 1sc in 1 st, 1sc decrease in next 2 sts, alternate, join in beg ch.
39 Repeat Round **38**.
40 1sc decrease in each 2sts around and slip stitch to close. Fasten off.

Making the arms
Use more flesh tone thread.
1 ch5 and join with a slip stitch to make a circle.
2 ch1. 1sc in each stitch, join in beg ch.
3-15 Repeat Round **2**. Do not fasten off.

Making the fingers
Start from the arm with the spool of thread attached; chains are fingers.
1 ch3. work 1sc into next stitch on end of arm.
2 ch4. work 1sc into next stitch on end of arm.
3 ch3. work 1sc into next stitch and fasten off. Make 2nd arm and fingers.

 Bead Crochet Techniques

Working from a Storage Card

Use a small rectangular piece of stiff cardboard, approximately 2" x 3", with a slot cut at each end to store loose thread and strung beads when not working on the project. Transfer thread from the spool to the storage card first. When you stop crocheting, wind all the thread including the strung beads onto the storage card. See the illustration. Take the loop off the hook and enlarge it to put around the storage card and leave one edge in one of the slots. Then the loop will not come loose and will be ready for the hook next time you crochet. If you leave the beads strung on a spool, they tend to move all around and knot together. Use a pen to list the type of thread put on the storage card for reference. Keep storage cards with and without beads stacked in clear plastic containers that are not airtight. When you are ready to crochet, unwrap the thread with the strung beads plus about another 12" of thread. If you find your beads sneaking up to the piece you are working and no thread left, unwrap more thread from the storage card and gently push the beads farther down on the thread.

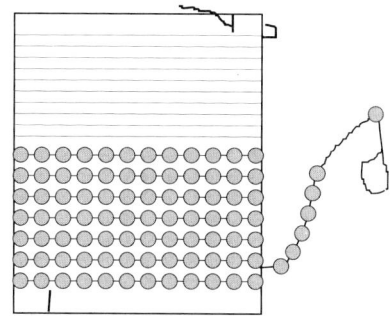
Thread and Beads Storage Card

Working from a Spool

You have a spool of thread, beads strung onto the thread and the loose end attached to the hook, ready to begin. As you pull up beads to work, you will eventually run out of thread. Gently push down the beads as you pull more thread up next to the hook from the spool. When you quit for the day, you will have an area of beads hanging loose from the main spool of thread. Thread often knots up between the beads and you have a mess the next day. Use the Storage Card method or take a safety pin and stick it through the loop you had on your hook. Then take a small plastic bag and roll the strung beads and thread around it with the safety pin sticking from the loop. Stick the safety pin into the plastic bag. This should keep the beads and thread secure.

Adding and Joining Thread

Joining New Thread When you have 2 loops of the old thread left, use the hook to pull in the new thread and work a few stitches of the new thread over the old end. Do not cut off the old thread ends until you are sure they will not be needed later.

Adding New Thread Crochet instructions say never fasten off to add new thread. However, when working tiny projects, many with bead stitches, the joining method does not always work. If you run out of thread, put the safety pin where you stopped and fasten off. Add new thread by making a slip knot for the hook. Then put the hook through the next stitch on the crocheted piece, yarnover and pull the hook back through the loop on the hook above the slip knot. See the illustration. Now the thread is attached. Continue to crochet. Weave the loose end of thread into the piece after you have crocheted a line of stitches. Use this technique when you run out of

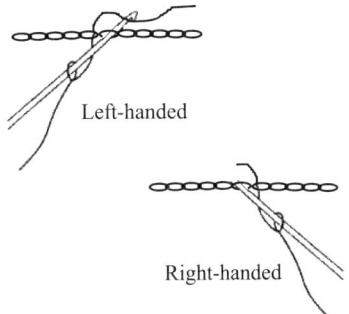
Left-handed

Right-handed

beads and need to add beads and thread or when you want to switch from crochet to another technique and back to crochet, such as beading or needlework.

Pre-stringing Beads

Use a twisted wire needle to pre-string beads. Take the needle through part of a strand of

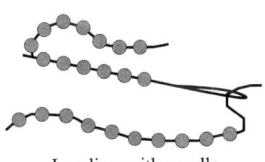
Loading with needle

beads on a hank and pull the beads from the strand onto the needle, stringing several at a time. See the illustration above. Beads can also be transferred from a strand directly to the crochet thread. Make a slip knot on the end of a bead strand from the hank and put the crochet thread end through the loop of the slip knot. Pull

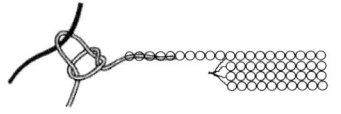
Loading without needle

the slip knot firm. Begin transferring beads from the strand to the crochet thread. See the illustration below. The bead strands often break and some bead holes are not large enough for the crochet thread. String these beads separately. If several beads strung and one "bad bead" is in the group (broken or chipped), use small pliers to break it. Place the pliers around one side of the bead, away from the thread in the bead hole and use the other hand to hold the thread away from the pliers while breaking the bead. Use safety glasses or shut your eyes for protection from flying glass pieces. Do not string more than 2 yards of beads at a time or the thread will begin to fray from the beads being moved back and forth. String beads and add new thread as needed.

53

Adding Beads to Crochet

Beads can be added to chain stitches, single crochet, double crochet and half double crochet. Add beads before or after any yarnover in a stitch. More than 1 bead can be added in a stitch. Add beads before or after every yarnover. Make a sampler of all bead placements in stitches for reference.

For all bead stitches: As soon as you add a bead, give the thread a tug, pulling the hook taut so the bead sits on the outside of the crochet piece and does not pull through to the inside that is facing you. Beads pull through if the loops behind them are too big. Smaller hooks make smaller loops that keep the beads in place. You will run out of thread when crocheting with beads. The beads will end up in front instead of thread. Push the beads down towards the spool or storage card and keep 12" of thread in front to work.

For chains: Make a slip knot, then pull up a bead next to the slip knot and yo behind the bead, capturing the bead in the chain. See the left and right-handed bead chain stitch illustrations. You now have 1 bead chain. Crochet 1 bead in each chain for the number of chains desired. See the bead chain illustration.

For single crochet: String some beads onto crochet thread. Then make group of sc stitches in a circle. See the sc circle illustration. Put the crochet hook through the next stitch for a sc, pull up the nearest bead on the thread and push it snug against the crocheted stitches. Yo behind the bead and pull a loop through. See left and right-handed bsc illustrations. Then yo again and draw through both loops on the hook. The bsc is complete and the bead is attached. Continue until finished. Use this bead placement for all the projects requiring bsc stitches. Beads can also be placed on after the first yo of a sc .

For half double crochet: Yo and pull up a stitch, then push your bead snug next to the crocheted stitches, then yo behind the bead and complete the hdc stitch. Continue until finished. You can also add the bead before the 1st yo and after the 2nd yo. Projects indicate placement.

For double crochet: Place the bead before or after any yo or after each yo. Projects indicate placement.

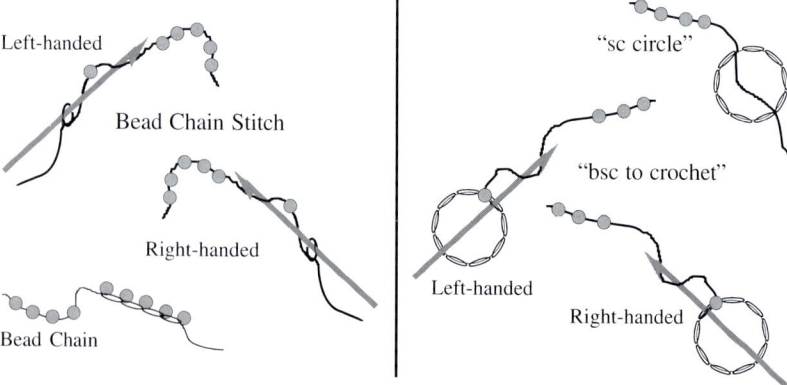

Left-handed

Bead Chain Stitch

Right-handed

Bead Chain

"sc circle"

"bsc to crochet"

Left-handed

Right-handed

Fastening/Tying Off Thread

Fastening off thread when:
- you are finished crocheting and want to sew in the thread that is looped on the hook;
- you have run out of beads and need to add new thread;
- you want to change to different thread or beads and do not want to run an auxiliary thread along with your current thread.

Widen the loop the crochet hook is in until it is a 6" loop. Take scissors and cut through the middle at the top of the loop. Pull the spool or storage card away from the crocheted piece. One loose thread will stick out of the crocheted piece. Put a sewing needle through the loose thread and sew into the item. Follow the crochet stitches already made until the thread is taut and will not come out. Cut off the excess thread. If you are adding new thread and beads and continuing where you fastened off, put a safety pin in the stitch right before that loose thread as a guide to begin again.

Tying off thread: If you are finishing or embellishing a crocheted piece using beading or sewing threads, follow the crochet stitches in one direction, then stitch in the opposite direction until the thread is taut before cutting off the excess. You can also use clear nail polish or the **Bic Trick**, pg.17, on beading thread ends.

Using Auxiliary Thread

Auxiliary thread can be used for many purposes. If you want to use a thicker fiber in a project that the beads will not fit through, string them on a thinner thread. Take both strands together and make the slip knot. Then begin crocheting with both threads. When you want a bead included, pull it up on the auxiliary thread and add it. If the beads are strung on a neutral or matching color to the thicker fiber, the thread will not show when you finish crocheting. If your beads are on a metallic or fancy thread it will appear as decorative between the thicker fiber. You can also add auxiliary thread without any beads as additional decoration to the fiber you are crocheting. Metallic threads can be included; however, when three or more are combined they can knot. Auxiliary thread can be used anytime and added in specific areas; add or join thread and fasten off each time as needed. Small beads can also be added on metallic threads.

Adding Beads between Beads

Embellish a crocheted item by adding beads between the crocheted beads. Example; use beading thread and a sharps needle, size 11 or 12 and add size 11 seed beads to a crocheted bead that is composed of size 6 or 8 seed beads. Take 60" of beading thread, thread the needle and double the thread. Either knot the thread and pull it through from the inside of the piece to the front or weave the thread through the crochet stitches on the piece until taut. Decide where to begin and put the needle through a bead on the crocheted piece, then string 2 to 3 small beads on and go through another bead on the crocheted piece. Add a few beads or larger loops of 5 or more beads for big loops. Tie off when finished.

Preparing Crochet for Bead or Fiber Attachment

You can add any beading technique to the edge of your thread or bead crocheted piece. When you finish a line of crochet and want to begin a different technique, fasten off. You should be able to start beading on the last line of crochet stitches. If the crochet thread is thick, you may have to make small stitches with sewing thread over the crochet thread around the edge of the piece and then bead from those stitches. If you made more stitches than needed for the first line of beads, skip those stitches not required. If some stitches are too tight to get the hook under, use a tapestry or sewing needle to loosen them up. When you have finished beading and want to crochet again, the last line of beading stitches should be firm enough for the hook to go under and not pull out stitches. Use sewing thread to stitch a second line of thread over the beading thread for strength if required.

Then take your crochet hook under those stitches to begin. Follow the directions for **Adding and Joining Thread,** pg. 53, to attach your crochet thread with a hook before beginning to crochet. If you are working from a heavy bead loomed piece, reinforce the edges of the bead loom pieces with sewing or thicker thread before hooking into it so the loomed beads will not become loose along the edges. Make crochet liners onto other beading techniques, such as a peyote bag, by stitching sewing thread over the last line of beading thread on the top of the bag opening and then use **Adding and Joining Thread** to attach your crochet thread with a hook. Make small tube purses with fancy ribbon by preparing both ends for crochet using the same methods. Attach crochet to any fabric by first making a line of stitches for the hook.

Decreasing Stitch with Beads

Standard single crochet decreases are not good for decreasing with beads. The thread shows between beads in the decrease. Skipping stitches will leave holes. Make bsc decreases with less thread showing this way: Take the hook through one stitch from the side facing you, go back through the next stitch from the opposite direction. See left and right-handed illustrations. Now pull up a bead, then yo behind the bead, pulling the hook through both stitches. Yo again through the two loops on the hook to finish. Take the hook under both loops in each stitch if they are loose. To decrease in hdc with beads, complete the first yo and then follow the bsc decrease instructions. Make a few samples for reference. Use standard sc decreases in thread without beads.

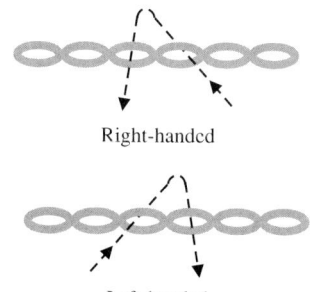

Right-handed

Left-handed

Making a Crocheted Strap

To make a chain stitch necklace/strap directly onto a purse, do not fasten off when you finish crocheting. Most purses in the round finish right near the opening where a strap could go. Take a hook and begin the chain with the same thread as the purse. Make the strand long enough to put over your head and remove easily. It needs tight uniform chains, especially if you are adding beads. When you finish the chain stitch strap, take the other end back to the purse and place it across from where the beginning strap sets on the purse. Take a sewing needle and stitch that end onto the purse and tie off. Double the width of the strap by making one chain at the end of the strap, turn and make single crochet stitches or slip stitches into the chain stitches before fastening off. Then go to the opposite side to attach the strap. Make straps with or without beads. Start with a shorter crochet strap and add a button on the end. Crochet a second strap and fasten off. Add a loop of thread or thin braid on the end as a closure for the button and tie off.

Making a Braid

Decide the braid length required to add fiber knots or a crochet bead on the end, fit around your neck, room for the purse on the end and be able to remove it over your head. Example: An average length is 30" plus 6" more for the purse to hang on and pull open; plus 2" for a knot or bead on the end and 2"extra as the braiding pulls fiber in a little; for a total length of 40". Make the braid with crochet thread using 3 strands 40" each for the braid. Knot 3 threads together about 5" from the cut ends, put a T-pin into that knot and attach the T-pin to a firm surface for working. Begin braiding next to the T-pin and continue until you have 5" of loose thread left. Follow illustration below, going left to right. Take the T-pin out of the knotted end and put a sewing needle through the loose thread end without the knot. Now you are ready to attach your braid to bags and decorative beads. Add more strands for thicker braids. This is a basic braid technique.

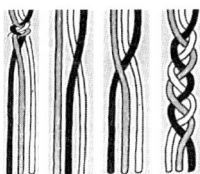

Braiding Steps

Making Bead Loops

Make a shaggy bag, bead or embellishment by adding loops of beads instead of one bead to a single crochet stitch. Example. Put the hook in the next stitch of the piece and pull up five beads. Yo behind the 5 beads and pull a loop through. Then make a second yo and pull the thread through both loops on the hook. Now you have a bead loop sticking out. Brace the bead loop against #3 finger of your other hand while completing the yo behind the loop. Make bead loops the same size or start with larger loops and decrease to a smaller loops on bags and dolls. Longer bead loops are more to difficult to work the hook behind and finish the stitch.

Embellishing with Beads

Embellishing Cords Purchase a length of cord made of fiber that is twisted or a mesh of thin cords. Use a sewing needle and thread to stitch back and forth over each end of the cord to keep threads from unraveling. Then sew a button on one end and a loop of soutache or thin cord on the other end as a closure for the button. Put a size 11 or 12 sharps needle on about 70" of beading thread, double the thread and knot the end. Take the beading thread through one end of the cord near the button or loop closure; twice if necessary for the thread to be taut. String on a bead and take the needle directly through the thick cord and come out the other side. Put on another bead, go directly through the cord and out. See the illustration. Your embellishment should spiral as you work toward the other end. When you have only 3" of thread left, weave in through the thick cord and tie off. Then add thread. Continue until you have embellished all the cord. See illustration.

Embellishing Beads, Purses and Dolls Embellish with beads on any crochet item using beading thread, sharps needles and seed beads. Follow the same embellishing directions as above for preparing the thread. Attach the thread near the area you want to embellish. Then string on the number of beads for embellishing and stitch into the crocheted surface. Bring the thread back out where you want the next embellishment to appear. When you are finished, weave the thread through the crochet stitches and tie off. Use a beading needle if your embellishment includes long loops of beads.

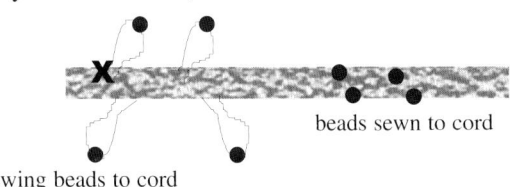

sewing beads to cord

beads sewn to cord

Adding Rings

Sewing on Rings: You can add glass, gemstone, metal, or other type rings to crochet using crochet, topstitching or sewing thread. Thread a sewing needle, go into the crochet piece and stitch a few times until the thread is taut. Then string on a ring and sew through it and into the crochet piece until it is secure and tie off.

Crocheting on Rings: This technique takes more time but the rings become a permanent part of the crocheted piece. First check to see if the ring holes are smaller than the strung beads, if they are, then make sure the rings are in front of strung beads before you begin. Then attach the thread with a hook to the piece in the area where you want the first ring to go. See **Adding - Joining Thread,** pg.53. Put a hook in the next stitch and bring the first ring up next to the hook. Take the hook to the side of the ring, yo and pull a loop through. See the left and right-hand illustrations. Now there are two loops on the hook. Make a 2ⁿᵈ yo and bring the hook through both loops finishing the sc. Now the ring is attached. See the illustration. Place a hook in the next stitch and continue working single crochet stitches from the last ring to the next area you want to place a ring. Then repeat the process until all the rings are attached. If you are working in rounds, finish with single crochet stitches and join with a slip stitch in the beginning stitch. This technique creates a small attractive ridge around purse openings. Use this technique to add rings to rows or rounds.

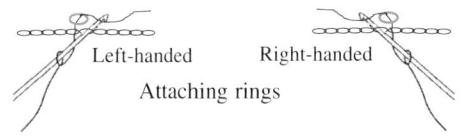

Left-handed   Right-handed
Attaching rings

Ring attached to crochet

Covering Rings

Covered Rings can be used as purse handles, jewelry or embellishments. Follow the right-handed and left-handed steps illustrated below.
1. Make a slip knot, take the hook through the ring, yo with thread outside the ring and bring the hook back through the ring and loop above the slip knot.
2. The thread is attached and the hook is outside the ring. With the hook outside the ring and thread through the ring on the opposite side, yo and bring the thread through the loop on the hook outside the ring. Now the ring is ready for continuous sc stitches.
3. Take the hook through the ring, yo, bring the hook back outside the ring; yo through 1 loop on the hook, then yo again through both loops on the hook outside the ring to complete 1sc. One yo is required to position the hook before beginning each sc.
4. The hook is outside the ring again and ready for the next sc.

Continue this technique and join at the end with a slip stitch to the beginning stitch. Then sew the ring to the piece. You can also string beads on the thread and add a bead or bead loop each time you make a sc stitch. Pull up the bead or bead loop and attach before the last yo.

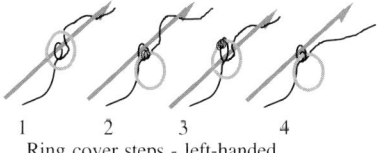

1   2   3   4
Ring cover steps - left-handed

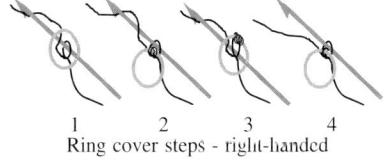

1   2   3   4
Ring cover steps - right-handed

Adding Fiberfill

Use fiberfill to stuff beads, dolls and embellishments. Pull tiny pieces of fiberfill apart and stuff into the piece. Use a tapestry needle or long pointed tool to push down the stuffing. Pack the piece tight or loose for the desired effect. Stuff beads when the first half is crocheted and stuff each doll piece as you crochet it.

Adding Lining to Bags

Lining Bags with Fabric: Most antique crochet and knitted bags were lined with silk, satin or other soft fabrics. Beige, white and other light colors were frequently used with the exception of black bags in which case a black lining was usually the choice. Today you can use any color you like. I prefer a traditional look and use several shades of beige and white silk fabrics. **The Sweet Dream** and **The Delicious Duo** include optional lining. You need the length and width of the purse plus fabric to turn under to keep from unraveling. Figure the length and width of the purse plus 3/8" added around the whole piece. Cut a piece of fabric for lining, turn under the 3/8" edge and iron the piece. This will keep the edges flatter. Now place the lining on top of the crocheted purse side without beads. Use silk pins to hold the lining while you stitch it to the purse. Use a sharps needle and beading thread or thin sewing needle and thread. Double the thread and make a knot in the end and sew it to the inside of the purse. Then bring the needle out to the purse edge where you want to begin attaching the lining. Take your thread through the 3/8" portion of the lining but not through to the outside. Then take your needle back into the crocheted piece and out. Make your next stitch the same way and very close to the last one. The stitches should be very small and not visible on the outside lining. Linings for 2 pieces are made the same way and each piece attached to the purse before it is sewn together. Round linings also use the 3/8" additional fabric and may have to be stitched with tiny pleating in the back if the circular fabric pieces pucker.

Using Buckram and Ultrasuede

Buckram can be used inside tiny purse lids or spliced between two pieces of ultrasuede prior to the edges of ultrasuede being crocheted. Buckram is used as a stiffener between other surfaces. Cut buckram pieces a little smaller than the item it will be spliced between. Buckram does not have to be sewn down; the ultrasuede on the outside will be sewn to the beaded piece with the buckram in between. Most fabric stores stock buckram.

Ultrasuede is a final finish or liner inside purses and lids, jewelry and clothing. Ultrasuede can be a final finish on the outside of an item that is part ultrasuede and part crochet. For lining, cut the ultrasuede the same size as the crocheted piece. Use sewing thread and needle or a sharps needle and beading thread to attach the ultrasuede to the piece. Make a beaded or crocheted edge. Use an awl to make holes in ultrasuede before crocheting. Substitute soft thin leather for ultrasuede. Most fabric stores offer buckram and ultrasuede. Most leather supply companies offer thin leathers.

Making a Crochet Bezel for a Cabochon

To crochet around cabochons or buttons on a surface, first prepare the surface for crochet. If you are capturing a button, stitch the button to the surface before you begin. If you are capturing a cabochon, you can use a dab of glue to hold the cabochon down but first read **Glue and Fibers**, pg.18. A fabric marker can also be used to draw an outline around the cabochon. Use sewing needle and thread to make small stitches on the surface in a line that is just outside the cabochon shape and tie off. See the illustration. Also check **Preparing Crochet for Bead or Fiber Attachment**, pg.56. Then follow directions for **Adding and Joining Thread**, pg.53, and attach the thread with the hook. Now you are ready to build a bezel around the cabochon with sc stitches. If you are including beads in the bezel, pre-string them. Put the hook into the first stitch, pull up a bead, yo behind the bead and finish the bsc. Make bsc stitches around the cabochon and finish with a slip stitch in the beginning bsc stitch. Then ch1 and continue another round of bsc, decreasing when necessary to make a snug bezel around the cabochon joining with a slip stitch in the beginning chain. Fasten off. You can also spiral instead of using slip stitches and beginning chains. The number of rounds you need will depend on the cabochon height. If the cabochon is not attached to a specific piece, see **Using Buckram and Ultrasuede**, pg.60, and **Pins and Pendants**, pg.62, for finishing the back. The cabochon should fit tight in the bezel and not slip out. See examples on the centerfold page and **The Bead Fairy**.

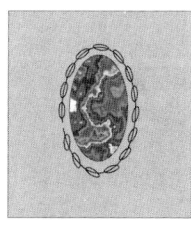

Crochet Bezel Around a Cabochon

Crocheting Consecutive Flat Bead Rows

Flat crocheted pieces are usually crocheted in one direction, then a chain made and the piece turned and worked in the opposite direction. When applying beads in every row, the piece must be worked using a different method. Make a row of standard bsc. When you are at the end of that row, ch1, turn the piece so you are facing that bead row. Put the hook behind the thread with strung beads. From the bead side facing you, put the hook through the first stitch in the previous row. Yo behind the bead and pull a loop through. Now you have 2 loops on the hook plus the loop with a bead on the back side. Use a finger to push the bead to the front and the thread loops behind the bead. Now yo again and pull the hook through all the loops on the hook. Continue to the end of the row. Then ch1 and turn the piece and begin the next standard bsc row. Use the same method for bead loops in consecutive rows. Try making **The Sweet Dream** with consecutive bead rows. Stitching in one direction in consecutive rows is a reverse sc stitch.

Making Crochet Pins and Pendants

Make pendants or pins with groups of crocheted beads, Scrunchies, Scroodles, Twisties or Clusters.

Pins: Crochet 3 to 5 pieces and stitch them together on the pin back side. Use a sewing needle and thread or sharps needle and beading thread to attach the pin. Ultrasuede can also be used to back the pieces before attaching the pin. Cut two pieces of ultrasuede into a shape and cut a piece of buckram a little smaller to fit between them. Stitch around the two pieces of ultrasuede with the buckram inside and attach the decorative side to the front and the pin to the back side. Sew bead loops around the ultrasuede edge as additional decoration. When adding a cabochon and bezel to the ultrasuede front, use one thickness to prepare for the cabochon and make the bezel. Then put the buckram and second layer of ultrasuede on the back and continue using the same techniques.

Pendants: Crochet a large bead and close one end to make a pendant or use one of the purse patterns and decrease one end to become a large bead. When the bead or purse is crocheted halfway, fill it with a wooden bead or fiberfill for a firm shape. Bead loops can be added to the pendant as embellishment. Make a chain stitch and attach several Scrunchies, Scroodles, Clusters or Twisties to hang as a pendant. Use a loop of beads or fiber to hang your pendants.

Making Crochet Earrings

Crocheted Beads: Sew a size 6mm, 8 mm or drop bead on one end of a crocheted bead. Then sew through crocheted stitches to the opposite end. Make a chain stitch loop from one side to the other and fasten off. Attach an earring finding onto the loop.

Scrunchies and Scroodles: Sew them onto earring pads.

Twisties and Clusters: Sew groups together and attach to earring pads or hang from earring studs/wires.

Mini Crocheted Purses: Make purses with size 16 and smaller seed beads. Then crochet or string a loop of seed beads at the top of the purses and attach earring findings.

Making Twisties

Make **Twisties** with or without beads in flat rows. Example: String 40 seed beads and chain 20. Now ch1 and turn, then work 1bsc under both loops of each previous chain. The chain will begin to twist. If you want more twist, skip a stitch here and there in the row. If you want less twist, add 2bsc in a stitch instead of 1bsc. If you want tentacles like **Mr. Tentacles**, the squid in the centerfold, string 20 seed beads in one color for the chain and 20 seed beads in a second color for the bsc stitches on the back. You can also slip stitch the beads for a tighter stitch but they are difficult to control.

Bibliography

Calder, Louisa and Mary Konior, **Louisa Calder's Creative Crochet**, Penguin Books, 1979

Coats & Clarks Book No. 170-D, **Learn How Book - Knitting, Crocheting, Tatting, Embroidery**, Coats & Clark's Sales Corp., 1975

Coats & Clark Book No 1403, **Crochet Made Easy,** Coats & Clark, 1993

Coburn, Kate, **Crocheting With Beads**, KTB Publishing, 1996

Coburn, Kate, **Tubes, Crocheting With Beads**, KTB Publishing, 1996

Dooner, Kate, **A Century of Handbags**, Schiffer Publishing Ltd., 1993

Elbe, Barbara E., **Back to Beadin,'** B.E.E. Publishing, 1996

Emma Post Barbour's New Bead Book, National Trading Co., 1924

Ettinger, Roseann, **Handbags**, Schiffer Publishing Ltd., 1991

Gerson, Roselyn, **Vanity Bags & Purses**, Collector Books, 1994

Haertig, Evelyn, **More Beautiful Purses**, Gallery Graphics Press, 1990

Irish Crochet Technique and Projects, The Priscilla Publishing Co., 1984

Kliot, Jules & Kaethe, Editors, **Bead Work**, Second Edition, Lacis Publications, 1996

Kliot, Jules & Kaethe, Editors, **Crochet Novelties from Turn-of-the Century Sources**, Lacis Publications, 1996

Mountford, Debra, Editor, **The Harmony Guide To Crocheting Techniques and Stitches**, Lyric Books Limited, 1986

Paludan, Lis, **Crochet, History & Technique**, Interweave Press, Inc., 1995

Priscilla Bead Work Book, The Priscilla Publishing Co., 1912

Schwartz, Lynell K., **Vintage Bags At Their Best**, Schiffer Publishing Ltd., 1995

Sommer, Elyse and Mike, **A New Look at Crochet Using Basic Stitches to Create Modern Designs**, Crown Publishers, Inc., 1975

Weiss, Rita, **Complete Guide to Thread Crochet**, American School of Needlework, Inc., ASN Publishing, 1994

Your miniature and amulet purses can last for a hundred years or longer with the exception of the straps. For stronger straps, string the beads on Soft-Flex^{tm} wire and use the techniques in **Beadwrangler's Hands On Bead Stringing** Book. Make Why-Knot necklaces to display them and move them between necklaces.

Bead and Fiber Organizations

Crochet Guild of America
P.O. Box 8043
Rolling Meadows, IL 60008-8043
Phone 847-776-7941 (9AM-5PM CST)
email:CGOA@crochet.org
website http://www.crochet.com

Bead Societies
For a complete list of bead societies, check "Lists" at www.beadwrangler.com or check the Lapidary Journal Bead Annual (October issue).

Beadwrangler's Hands On Series

Beadwrangler's Hands On Bead Stringing
Beadwrangler's Hands On Crochet with Beads and Fiber

Coming soon…..
Beadwrangler's Hands On Loom Weaving with Beads and Fiber
Beadwrangler's Hands On Embellishment with Beads and Fiber
Beadwrangler's Hands On Crochet II - More Bead and Fiber Projects

Beadwrangler's Bead and Fiber Junction

Lydia's Website on the Internet
Over 400 pages of bead and fiber fun!
Free Workshops
News, Events & Tips
Special Features & Guest Articles
Resources, Information & Inspiration
www.beadwrangler.com